# SACAGAWEA

**Recent Titles in Greenwood Biographies**

# SACAGAWEA

## A Biography

April R. Summitt

GREENWOOD BIOGRAPHIES

GREENWOOD PRESS
WESTPORT, CONNECTICUT • LONDON

**Library of Congress Cataloging-in-Publication Data**

Summitt, April R.
    Sacagawea : a biography / April R. Summitt.
        p. cm. — (Greenwood biographies, ISSN 1540–4900)
    Includes bibliographical references and index.
    ISBN: 978–0–313–34628–6 (alk. paper)
  1. Sacagawea.   2. Shoshoni women—West (U.S.)—Biography.
3. Shoshoni Indians—West (U.S.)—Biography.   4. Lewis and Clark
Expedition (1804–1806).   5. West (U.S.)—Discovery and exploration.
6. Lewis and Clark Expedition (1804–1806)—Miscellanea.   7. West
(U.S.)—Discovery and exploration—Miscellanea.   I. Title.
    F592.7.S123S85   2008
    978.04'9745740092—dc22
    [B]        2008017543

British Library Cataloguing in Publication Data is available.

Library of Congress Catalog Card Number: 2008017543
ISBN: 978–0–313–34628–6
ISSN: 1540–4900

First published in 2008

Greenwood Press, 88 Post Road West, Westport, CT 06881
An imprint of Greenwood Publishing Group, Inc.
www.greenwood.com

Printed in the United States of America

∞

The paper used in this book complies with the
Permanent Paper Standard issued by the National
Information Standards Organization (Z39.48–1984).

10   9   8   7   6   5   4   3   2   1

*For my Mother Connie,*
*for always being there*

# CONTENTS

*Photo essay follows page 66*

# SERIES FOREWORD

In response to high school and public library needs, Greenwood developed this distinguished series of full-length biographies specifically for student use. Prepared by field experts and professionals, these engaging biographies are tailored for high school students who need challenging yet accessible biographies. Ideal for secondary school assignments, the length, format and subject areas are designed to meet educators' requirements and students' interests.

Greenwood offers an extensive selection of biographies spanning all curriculum-related subject areas including social studies, the sciences, literature and the arts, history and politics, as well as popular culture, covering public figures and famous personalities from all time periods and backgrounds, both historic and contemporary, who have made an impact on American and/or world culture. Greenwood biographies were chosen based on comprehensive feedback from librarians and educators. Consideration was given to both curriculum relevance and inherent interest. The result is an intriguing mix of the well known and the unexpected, the saints and sinners from long-ago history and contemporary pop culture. Readers will find a wide array of subject choices from fascinating crime figures like Al Capone to inspiring pioneers like Margaret Mead, from the greatest minds of our time like Stephen Hawking to the most amazing success stories of our day like J. K. Rowling.

While the emphasis is on fact, not glorification, the books are meant to be fun to read. Each volume provides in-depth information about the subject's life from birth through childhood, the teen years, and adulthood.

A thorough account relates family background and education, traces personal and professional influences, and explores struggles, accomplishments, and contributions. A timeline highlights the most significant life events against a historical perspective. Bibliographies supplement the reference value of each volume.

# INTRODUCTION

Who was Sacagawea? Although many books have been written about this woman over the years, she remains a mystery. What little we do know about her short life comes from third-person mentions in the journals kept by the Lewis and Clark expedition of 1804–1806. In fact, very few people knew about her or paid much notice to the "Squaw" mentioned in the journals until the centennial of the expedition. In 1902, Eva Emory Dye, a novelist of the romantic west, wrote a novel about the Lewis and Clark expedition and Sacagawea entitled *The Conquest*. Published just before the centennial celebration, her book became very popular and inspired a good number of statues, celebrations, and other sorts of commemorations.

Suddenly, this obscure figure of a quiet American Indian girl rose to become a heroine of grand proportions. Sacagawea (or *Sacajawea* as most people spelled it) was lauded as an important role model for American women and girls, a valuable asset for the great expedition west, and a key figure in early American history. Soon she was called the guide for Lewis and Clark, although in truth she only served as an interpreter. Statues of Lewis and Clark soon would include the "Indian guide" with papoose on her back, pointing the way through the western wilderness. School children read stories about her, performed plays that featured her, and listened to speeches that praised her and raised her in importance even above another lauded Native American woman, Pocahontas.

The objective of this book is to create an accurate account of Sacagawea's life as far as we can find evidence and discuss her true value to the Lewis and Clark expedition. However, Sacagawea as myth is just as important as Sacagawea as fact. Thus, I will also examine the role she has played in the American psyche over the years and evaluate some of the stories that were quite widely believed through the late nineteenth and early twentieth centuries. One of the most interesting stories is that Sacagawea actually lived a long life and died in 1884 on the Wind River Reservation in Wyoming. It is not a simple task to answer the question, who was Sacagawea? Even though there have been at least a dozen historical works written that try to answer that question, many mysteries remain. Some of these questions will continue to inspire theories and stories, as the impact of this small Shoshone woman reaches down to us through the years.

Although Sacagawea has long been considered an American heroine, few people have been able to agree even on something as simple as the spelling of her name. In the Lewis and Clark journals, the only real historical records written during her life, most references called her "Toussaint's wife," "Charbonneau's woman," "Charbonneau's squaw or squar," or "the Indian woman." In a few places, Lewis attempted to spell out her name, perhaps written into the journals after the journey. In one entry, Clark spelled it "Sah-kah-gar-we-a."[1] Probably because of this and other similar references, the most common spelling of her name is *Sacagawea*, as used in this volume. In 1910, the U.S. Bureau of American Ethnology settled on this spelling and used it for the minting of the dollar coin in her honor.

Another common spelling is *Sakakawea*, meaning "bird woman" in Hidatsa. This spelling is used throughout North Dakota and by the Hidatsa people. The Hidatsa were the plains tribe that captured Sacagawea as a girl of 12 and with whom she lived until she married trader Toussaint Charbonneau. The Hidatsa claim this is the correct spelling because of its meaning and since Meriwether Lewis referred to her name as meaning "bird woman." While the pronunciation would have the same hard *g* or *k* sound, the use of the *k* conforms more to Hidatsa spellings. A third spelling, *Sacajawea* with a *j*, was very popular until the late twentieth century. Nicholas Biddle, the first person to edit and publish the journals of the expedition, spelled her name with a *j*, and subsequent authors like the popular novelist Eva Emery Dye and historian Grace Hebard also spelled the name with a *j*. The Lemhi Shoshone people today mostly prefer this spelling, even though some modern linguists have argued that this spelling would not have been comprehensible to Shoshone speakers.

To write this book, I have used a number of important sources and compared the stories of other authors about Sacagawea. The most important source is the journals of Lewis and Clark, as well as those of three other members of the expedition: Sergeants John Ordway and Patrick Gass, and

Private Joseph Whitehouse. Along with the journals of William Clark and Meriwether Lewis, these records provide the only real documents about Sacagawea. There have been several editions of the journals published over time. Nicholas Biddle and Paul Allen published the first edition a few years after the journey in 1814. Biddle and Allen took the original 18 notebooks and condensed them into 2 volumes. It made the journals accessible to the reading public but collapsed each entry into a single one. Most references to Sacagawea were not included in this edition.

In the late nineteenth century, Elliott Coues published another edition of the journals. His version also collapsed the separate entries into single voices for each day and cut out the days that seemed unimportant, as had Biddle and Allen's version. Coues, however, added some commentary to the journals, sometimes using some direct quotes from the original journals along with some of his own opinions on members of the expedition, including Sacagawea. Although Dye's novel had not yet been published, renewed interest in the Lewis and Clark expedition and Sacagawea's role in it influenced Coues as he prepared his edition. He then continued throughout the journals to add annotations that drew contrasts between Sacagawea and her husband, Toussaint Charbonneau. By the end of the work, the reader has a vision of Charbonneau as completely inadequate and cruel, and Sacagawea as heroic, beautiful, and "one of the best mothers."[2]

Not many years later, Reuben Gold Thwaites edited a complete edition of the journals between 1904 and 1906. In his 8-volume edition, readers could finally access the complete journals of the five expedition members who kept records. For a very long time, the Thwaites edition was the best resource for accuracy and completeness. Published just in time for the centennial celebration of the expedition, it was available for researchers. Most writers, however, continued to look at the smaller compilations for inspiration for their articles and novels. In 1953, Bernard De Voto published another abridged edition of the journals, which remained the best brief version of the journals until 1964. That year, John Bakeless produced another abridged version of the journals from the Thwaites edition.

Most recently, Gary E. Moulton published the best and most complete edition of the journals in 13 volumes from 1983 to 2004. He also produced an abridged version in 2003 and in 2005; the University of Nebraska Press digitized Moulton's edition of the journals, providing online access to all the materials and commentary. The Moulton edition, while including footnotes and some commentary, seeks to provide the clearest version of the original journals without individual interpretations. Moulton's edition, both in print and digitized form, is the primary source for this biography.

The only other records about Sacagawea are contained in William Clark's papers, which he kept after the expedition while he served as governor of Missouri and, later, head of Indian relations west of the Mississippi. His personal papers contain a letter he wrote to Toussaint Charbonneau, asking him to come live in St. Louis after the expedition and to bring Sacagawea and their son. Some of Clark's account books record his expenses for raising Sacagawea's son and list members of the expedition and what happened to them. Clark makes note of Sacagawea's death in one of his record books.

Other than another record by a man in Fort Manuel, South Dakota, recording her death there in 1812, no other documents exist to inform us about Sacagawea. Most of what people have written about her is based on conjecture, rumor, and fiction. Still, her story is truly an amazing one, and even when the legends and exaggerations are stripped away, Sacagawea remains an important figure in American history and an American Indian woman who lived an extraordinary life.

In researching and writing this book, I am indebted to a number of people. I wish to thank Leslie Waggener and John Waggener, research librarians at the American Heritage Center at the University of Wyoming; and Ellen Welty, Mike Wirtz, and Danielle Carlock at Arizona State University's Polytechnic Campus Library. My colleagues and Chair Duane Roen at ASU's Humanities and Arts Department, and Dean David Schwalm of the School of Applied Arts and Sciences also supported me. I also want to thank my friends and family and especially my husband, Don Fixico, and stepson, Keytha Fixico, who inspire me every day.

## NOTES

1. William Clark, April 7, 1805, in *The Journals of the Lewis and Clark Expedition*, ed. Gary E. Moulton (Lincoln: University of Nebraska Press, 1983–2001). Also available at http://lewisandclarkjournals.un.edu/index.html.

2. Elliot Coues, *History of the Expedition under the Command of Lewis and Clark*. 3 vols. (1893; reprint, New York: Dover Publications, 1965), 1:232.

# TIMELINE: EVENTS IN THE LIFE OF SACAGAWEA

1659  The Charbonneau family arrives in Montreal from France.

1673  Jacques Marquette and Louis Joliet discover the mouth of the Mississippi River.

1720  Horses and European goods arrive in the Rockies from Spanish Southwest.

1767  Birth of Toussaint Charbonneau on March 20 in Boucherville, Quebec.

1788  Birth of Sacagawea of the Lemhi Shoshones near present-day Tendoy, Idaho.

1796  Toussaint lives with the Hidatsa in present-day North Dakota.

1800  Sacagawea captured by the Hidatsa at age 12 near the three forks of the Missouri River during a hunt. Toussaint Charbonneau, a French trader to the Hidatsa and Mandan, acquires her as his second wife a few years later.

1803  The Louisiana Purchase is acquired by the United States from France in May.

1804  On May 14, the Lewis and Clark expedition begins the first part of its journey up the Missouri River. They arrive at the Mandan villages in October.
      Sacagawea likely meets Meriwether Lewis and William Clark on November 4 when they hire her husband as an interpreter.

1805  Sacagawea gives birth to her first child, Jean-Baptiste Charbonneau, on February 11. William Clark helps deliver the baby.
      Sacagawea and her husband and child join the Corps of Discovery and head upstream on April 7.

On May 16, Sacagawea saves much of the corps' equipment and supplies when the boat she was riding in nearly capsizes.

On June 10, Sacagawea becomes dangerously ill but recovers after a few weeks.

On August 8, Sacagawea recognizes Beaverhead Rock and Three Forks and confirms that the expedition is on the right path to her people.

Sacagawea meets her brother Chief Cameahwait and her people on August 17 for the first time since her capture at age 12.

The expedition and Sacagawea finally see the Pacific Ocean for the first time in December.

1806    The Corps of Discovery leaves Fort Clapsot to begin the journey back home on March 23.

Jean-Baptiste becomes very ill on May 26 with what might have been mumps. He recovers in a few weeks.

In July, Sacagawea helps direct Clark to the Bozeman Pass (avoiding the Flathead Pass).

The expedition finally arrives back at the Mandan villages in August. Clark invites Sacagawea and her family to return to St. Louis with him, but they refuse.

The Corps of Discovery finally arrives back in St. Louis, their point of origin, on September 23.

1809    Meriwether Lewis dies on October 11.

1810    Toussaint Charbonneau, Sacagawea, and their children travel to St. Louis to accept William Clark's offer of help to begin a farm. Clark begins paying for and overseeing the education of Jean-Baptiste. They only stay three months.

1811    Sacagawea and Toussaint travel with the Missouri Fur Company from St. Louis upriver on April 2. Sacagawea is sickly.

1812    Sacagawea dies on December 20 at Fort Manuel in present-day South Dakota at the probable age of 25. Clark becomes guardian of her children.

1819    Toussaint is employed by the U.S. Indian Department Upper Missouri subagency.

1820    Clark sends Jean-Baptiste to a boarding school.

1823    Duke Fredrick Paul Wilhelm of Württemberg meets Jean-Baptiste while in the United States and takes him back to Germany.

1829    After traveling all over Europe and learning to speak German, French, and English, Jean-Baptiste returns to the United States.

1830    Jean-Baptiste joins the Roubidoux Fur Brigade in the Rocky Mountains.

1838 William Clark dies on September 1.
1839 Last record of Toussaint when he collects his final government pay in August.
1843 Probable year of Toussaint's death. In this year, Jean-Baptiste was allocated money from his father's estate.
1846 Jean-Baptiste accompanies the Kearny expedition to the Southwest.
1849 Jean-Baptiste participates in the California gold rush.
1852 Jean-Baptiste works as an assistant surveyor in Placer County, California.
1866 Jean-Baptiste dies of pneumonia in Danner, Oregon.

# Chapter 1

# SACAGAWEA OF THE SHOSHONES

There are more rivers and mountains named after Sacagawea than any other American woman. She has more statues and memorials to her than any other Native American. Her only rival in popularity and name recognition might be Pocahontas, another young native woman who died young. Both women are credited with helping the survival of Europeans who came to their homelands as colonists. Both women, however, are more mysterious to us than real. The myths we hold about them are perhaps unmatched by the realities we know little about. Yet, Sacagawea's name calls up many images of a brave, young Indian woman who guided the Lewis and Clark expedition, saving them from many perils. How much of this image is true? What is the legacy of Sacagawea's life? To answer these questions, we need to start at the beginning of what we know about this famous American woman.

It is almost impossible to start Sacagawea's story at any place other than her first meeting with Lewis and Clark. When she first met them at the Mandan villages in 1804, she was probably about 16 years old. There are no records about her earlier life except what she told Lewis and Clark while on their journey. Sacagawea told these men that she had been captured by Hidatsas as a little girl (probably about 12) while her tribe of Lemhi Shoshones were traveling across the Rocky Mountains. They were camped in the region of Three Forks where three rivers join to form the Missouri River. At this spot, near the present towns of Bozeman and Butte, Montana, Sacagawea was taken along with some other girls as her people came under attack.

Since we cannot know anything for sure about Sacagawea's childhood prior to her capture, the best we can do is to know something about what Shoshone life was like for most children of her age. There is quite a lot of information about the culture of those who will later be known as the Lemhi Shoshones. What was it like to grow up among the Shoshones? What did Sacagawea learn that gave her the courage and strength to survive the traumas of losing home and family? What shaped her to become brave enough as a young teenager to travel into the unknown carrying her first child on her back in only the company of men?

## THE LEMHI SHOSHONES

The word *Shoshone* applies to a large group of related people who all shared a common language and culture. While it is unclear what the word *Shoshone* actually means, this group was known to some tribes as Snake People and to others as Grass House People. In the centuries before Sacagawea's life, Shoshone people lived in various groups that would later band together. Three of these groups, the Salmon-eaters (Agaidikas), the Sheep-eaters (Tukudekas), and the Buffalo-eaters (Kucundikas) all lived in various parts of the present states of Idaho and Montana.[1] They first lived in grass houses made of woven grass mats attached to a framework of branches. Later, when they acquired the horse from the Comanches, they learned to hunt buffalo and began making skin houses like some of their Plains neighbors.

Some scholars say that the Shoshones moved into the plateau areas after originating in the Southwest basin, where they had previously relied on gathering wild roots, berries, and nuts for the majority of their diet.[2] As some Shoshones moved into areas near salmon-filled mountain streams, their diets changed significantly. Other scholars argue that the Shoshone people probably migrated down to the Salmon River area of Idaho from the northern Rockies in Canada.[3] The Lemhi Shoshones, however, have their own story. They believe they have always lived along the Salmon River and that they were given this land as their home. Like many other Native American peoples, the Lemhi Shoshones have stories they tell about how they were created.[4] Sacagawea would have grown up hearing about how Coyote had found a woman, had children with her, and had washed some of the many babies with his own hands. These babies would become the Shoshone people, while the others washed by the daughter and mother became other American Indian people.

The place where Sacagawea grew up was a place of water and canyons, of mountains and grasslands. Her people lived at the conjunction of the Lemhi and Salmon rivers in what is now Idaho. The Salmon River (known to the Lemhi Shoshones today as the River of No Return) ran through a canyon deeper than the Grand Canyon in Arizona. The land is rugged and steep, and the water swift. Since salmon was so abundant, the Lemhi Shoshones made it a staple of their diet. It is likely that Sacagawea saw her male family members fishing on an almost daily basis during spring, early summer, and fall when the salmon swam upstream to spawn. Very early, she probably learned ways to help her mother and older female family members prepare and dry fish to preserve it. It took all family members to manage the daily tasks necessary to gather and preserve food in preparation for the bitter cold of winter.

In one Shoshone story, Coyote saw a woman carrying a basket filled with water and salmon. Coyote tipped the woman's basket out, and where the water ran, it created rivers full of salmon. Soon, Coyote became tired of chasing salmon up and down the rivers, so he built a dam to hold them. After a time, however, the dam broke, so Coyote told the fish that they had to return to the mountains each year. One day, Coyote saw that someone had constructed a dam, blocking the salmon from returning to the mountains to spawn. Coyote found a way to break down the dam and allow the salmon to return to their spawning grounds.[5] Sacagawea must have heard this story many times and remembered it when helping with the fish.

Since it took many hands to manage the tasks necessary for survival, marriage was an important part of Shoshone culture. Even if marriages did not last very long, staying single was seldom a real option for Shoshone adults.[6] Thus, it was likely that Sacagawea's parents had long thought about potential mates for her. Apparently, they had made a choice and negotiated a price with a young man when Sacagawea was captured. Were the two friends and did they like each other? Sacagawea never mentioned any previous betrothals, although she later met her former betrothed. Once she was taken away from Shoshone life, she must have set aside any hopes she might have had about her previous marriage plans.

Other than the usual tasks of house making, preparing skins, finding wild foods, and preserving fish, Sacagawea listened to other stories about Coyote and his elder brother Wolf. She would have heard stories about Paona, the water baby that could be heard crying in the night, or Pandzoavits, the giant who also lived in the water. The Shoshones, like many other Native American tribes, had numerous stories about spirits and animals. They believed that animals, spirits, and other mystical beings were the equals of humans and that they could at times communicate with each other. Sacagawea would have heard the story about how the little chickadee had made the world in which she lived. She also would have listened to the howl of a coyote at night and remembered stories that assured her its howl was a good omen.

In the evenings, Sacagawea would also have heard the sounds of her father and male relatives gathered around a fire, gossiping and gambling. On special occasions, she would be allowed to watch and then participate in the dancing, followed by a day of feasting when there was enough food. Most of the time, however, the entire tribe was engaged in never-ending efforts to find and preserve food. There were likely many times that Sacagawea was hungry when she was growing up. Thus, she would have learned at a very young age how to find various kinds of berries and seeds and when they grew. She also would have known how to find wild carrots, thistle taproots, and other roots that could be eaten either raw or cooked. Sacagawea's knowledge eventually served the members of the Lewis and Clark expedition very well in supplementing their diets.

## NATIVE AMERICAN WOMEN

As a young girl, Sacagawea was bound for a life that valued women. Although her Shoshone society might have placed women in a somewhat lower position than men, women were respected throughout Native American culture. Historian Theda Purdue writes, "Native peoples honored mothers . . . by recognizing the social, economic, and political importance of their reproductive role."[7] As the bearer of children, women were respected and cared for throughout their lives. Women were also the ones who preserved food, cured skins, constructed the grass or skin houses, and gathered wild foods to supplement their diets. While men were important as hunters, fishers, and fighters, all members of the tribe understood the vital part that women played in basic survival, as well as their roles as mothers.

Native American women were also diplomats who helped communicate between groups inside and outside of the community. Sacagawea learned from her family the importance of relationships and would have eventually wielded considerable influence over even her male children. In some groups, Native American women had the power to appoint or depose male chiefs or leaders. In most societies, mothers continued to influence children, helping to shape the actions of the younger generation. Sacagawea might have been a powerful matriarch of a large Shoshone family had she stayed with her people and lived a long life. She would have given birth to her first child with the help of an older woman as a midwife. She would have stayed in seclusion for about a month after the birth of the child, and her husband would not have visited her or the child during this time. As it turned out, however, Sacagawea gave birth to her first child far away from the traditional help of the older women of her tribe.

After giving birth, a Shoshone mother would carry her baby around with her in a cradle board strapped to her back while she continued cleaning fish or hides, digging for roots, or gathering berries and seeds. Children would play with grandmothers of the village until becoming old enough to follow their mother's example, learning her skills. If a child were male, he would learn early to play war games or pretend buffalo hunts. Sacagawea's son would also have learned to listen to the stories of the old men of the village at night around the fire so that he could tell the stories one day to his children. Sacagawea's daughter would have learned to make clothing, repair grass or skin houses, and find and preserve food. She would have learned about natural medicines, about preserving good family relationships, and about the land and its stories.

## CAPTURE AND LIFE WITH THE HIDATSAS

When Sacagawea was about 12 years old, her people were traveling east through the mountains near her home when they were attacked by a group of Hidatsa people. She and a few other girls were captured and taken away to live with strangers. Although Sacagawea never told anyone how this experience felt to her, it must have been frightening. Whether or not she knew what to expect, her life with the Hidatsas would have been somewhat different than her life up until that point. Yet, if she became an adopted member of the Hidatsas, her life would follow very similar patterns to what she had known among her own people.

Among the Hidatsa, Mandan, and Arikara peoples of the northern plains, girls like Sacagawea would have entered womanhood at about the age of 13 or 14. Until that time, the life of a young girl would have been much the same as a Shoshone girl. Sacagawea would have learned much about agriculture since the Hidatsa people relied heavily on growing corn and other crops such as beans and squash. While the Hidatsas hunted buffalo and other game, they did not have the abundance of salmon that the Shoshones enjoyed near their home, so women became very knowledgeable farmers. They were responsible for all the agriculture, while the men took care of hunting, war, and politics. However, both gender groups held each other in mutual respect and helped each other in their tasks.

In both the Hidatsa and Mandan villages, women also constructed and maintained the lodges where they lived. Sacagawea would have learned

to make lodges of similar construction to that of the Shoshones—a framework made of poles and covered with woven grass mats. The Hidatsas and
Mandans covered these structures with earth to make the lodges warm
during the harsh winter snows. Women also cared for the lodges, sweeping
the dirt floors daily, and they did many other things including caring for
children, grinding corn, and preparing meals. The daily life of an American Indian woman was very busy, indeed.

Scholars suspect that Sacagawea lived as a captive with the Hidatsas
anywhere from six months to two years before she was sold to Toussaint
Charbonneau as a wife. One writer argued that she was Charbonneau's
prize won in a gambling game, but the writer's source is not considered
credible by most historians today.[8] Whatever happened to Sacagawea immediately upon arriving at the Hidatsa villages, one will never know for
sure. It was Hidatsa tradition (and likely Shoshone) to take captives as
spoils of war.[9] Sometimes, the Hidatsa leaders sent sons as captives to
other nations in order to secure an alliance. Such captives would have
been treated as adopted sons.

In the adoption pipe ceremony, both village groups would begin prepa-
rations for an elaborate ritual. Once all was ready, a daylong ceremony
began that would include the exchange of gifts and pledges on both sides.
An adopting man or woman would pledge to be a good father or mother
to the adoptee, while the adopted daughter or son would pledge their
loyalty and obedience. This kind of adoption practice was usually used to
cement trade and military alliances between tribes. A white trader named
Alexander Henry once observed an adoption pipe ceremony in which a
Cheyenne leader gave his son to be adopted by the Hidatsas. Such adop-
tions created important connections between villages and native peoples
of different tribes.[10]

Since adoption was commonplace among the Hidatsas, it is possible
that Sacagawea lived with a family much like an adopted daughter. However, she had not been willingly traded, but taken as a prize of war. Still,
Hidatsa tribal members today and other historical sources argue that even
war captives were adopted into the tribe as equal members. Sacagawea
could have become a daughter, in which case she would have worked
very hard with the mother of the warrior who captured her, much as she
would have done with her own mother. Women in both the Shoshone
and Hidatsa tribes lived their lives according to the seasons. In the spring,
women and girls prepared the soil, planted crops, and participated in important ceremonies designed to ensure good harvests. In the summer, the
women helped the men prepare for the summer hunts, skinned and butch-
ered the buffalo and other game, cured skins, and dried meat.

Autumn was a busy time of harvesting and preserving crops and storing them in deep holes or caches near the lodges. The early autumn was also when the trading fairs were held, and the women prepared their excess corn and other goods for the fairs. French and other native traders came to the fairs and exchanged much-needed goods. Since one of the most important trade goods for the Hidatsas was the extra corn they grew, the women held considerable power and influence over the well-being of the tribe. Sacagawea would have been inducted into one of the "age-grade societies" that provided organization and stability to Hidatsa villages. Each age group had specific ceremonial tasks assigned, and Sacagawea would have begun learning these traditions with her age-grade group as she reached puberty. As each season of the year approached, both men and women had specific ceremonies to attend to that would ensure supernatural assistance for their crops, the hunting parties, and even childbirth.[11]

As a young Hidatsa woman reached the age of 13 or 14, she was made ready for marriage, which was usually arranged by her family or guardians. If she had remained among the Hidatsas, Sacagawea likely would have given birth to her first child between the ages of 14 and 16 and would have earned a place in the age-grade society of young adult women. As an adult, she would have been expected to assume the duties of motherhood and care of the lodge in which she lived. She and her husband would likely have moved in with her adopted mother until enough children made it necessary to build their own lodge. Sacagawea would have constructed this lodge and governed the planting of her own gardens with the help of daughters and eventually daughters-in-law and granddaughters. Through the yearly cycles of planting and harvesting, birth and death, women of the plains developed strong bonds that enabled them to hand down knowledge through the generations. Sacagawea would have been proud of her legacy and might have earned the respect of her fellow Hidatsa women. As an older woman, she would have become an important leader of spiritual ceremonies and rituals and would have aided young women as they became wives and mothers.

In past years, outside observers assumed that American Indian women were grossly mistreated by their husbands and treated as virtual slaves. This perception comes from a misunderstanding of Native American culture. European traditions and culture held that agricultural work belonged to men and that women should stay inside the home whenever possible, although not many farm wives could really live up to this expectation. Thus, Euro-American observers assumed that American Indian men were lazy because they made the women do all of the farming and house building. Today, many scholars have effectively argued that women held a respected role in American Indian societies and even wielded some power as the primary producers of food and trade goods. Sacagawea would not have lived as a slave to an American Indian husband.

As it turned out, Sacagawea's short life was to be far different than most other Shoshone or Hidatsa women of her age and generation. Although the exact year is not known, sometime between 1799 and 1803, Sacagawea became the wife of Toussaint Charbonneau, the French fur trader. Although most sources say she was "sold" to him, it is likely that white observers misunderstood what was to the Hidatsas a common practice of trading goods for the right to marry. Frequently, the prospective groom gave horses to the family of the bride. Charbonneau might have given horses or some other goods and considered it a trade or purchase, while it is most likely that the Hidatsa family receiving the goods saw it as a "bride-price."[12]

Thus at the age of 16, when Sacagawea met Lewis and Clark at the Mandan village, she was an adult woman, married to a French trader, and soon to bear her first child. Although still a child by today's standards, Sacagawea was like other females of her age and well trained for her role as a woman of the plains. When she gave birth to her first child, a son, she was ready for motherhood, even though the first two years of it would be anything but typical.

If Sacagawea had stayed behind with the Mandans, her son, Jean-Baptiste, would have spent the first three months of his life wrapped tightly in a bundle of cloth or skins in a cradle board strapped on his mother's back. A few times a day, Sacagawea would have loosened his wrappings so that he could move and kick his little legs. Since it took almost nine months for the expedition to reach the Pacific Ocean and their winter camp at Fort Clapsot, Jean-Baptiste likely spent most of those first nine months wrapped and in a cradle board—six months longer than was usual. There is no evidence that this affected the little boy in any way; there were plenty of opportunities for the baby to move about and eventually even learn to crawl in the tent that he and his mother and father shared on the journey with Lewis and Clark.

Typically, the Mandan and Hidatsa people (probably also the Shoshone people) waited for 10 days before naming a child because it was common for infants to die before 10 days had passed. If a child died before receiving a name, the Plains people believed that the child's spirit returned to a spirit home where it would later be reborn. After the 10-day period, children were named according to their gender. If the child was a girl, she was given some kind of special name that would be hers the rest of her life. Women did not take on the names of their husbands in Plains cultures. If the child was a boy, he would receive a name for his childhood, and likely another one after he had participated in his first war party and perhaps even again after a particularly brave deed.

Sacagawea's son received the name Jean-Baptiste Charbonneau, a typical French name. We do not know if Sacagawea was happy about her son being named in the European fashion. Later during the expedition with Lewis and Clark, the men gave Jean-Baptiste nicknames, calling him the Dancing Boy and Pomp, Little Pomp, or Pompy. The latter nicknames referred either to Napoleon or to the Roman emperor Pompey. These affectionate names painted a picture of a little emperor who ruled their hearts if no other kingdoms. Clark would later name a large rock outlook after the youngster, calling it Pompy's Tower, just as a Roman emperor might have had a monument named in his honor.

As baby Jean-Baptiste grew older, Sacagawea would have made him other clothes to wear besides the wrapping cloths. He would have worn loose shirts made of soft skins during the day but would still have been wrapped at night. When they were at the fort near the Pacific for a long winter, Sacagawea probably made him his first real pair of moccasins and leggings made of skins. Among the Mandans, most young boys and girls received a buffalo robe at around the age of six. Jean-Baptiste probably received one also when he returned to living among the Mandans after the expedition, perhaps just before he went to St. Louis with his parents in 1809 at the age of five.

If his first year and a half of life had been in the Mandan villages, young Jean-Baptiste would have crawled and walked under the care of a grandmother when his mother was out working in the fields or curing hides. By the time he was walking, his first real toy would have been an educational one—a bow and arrow. Thus, little boys grew up holding the major tools of their lives and learning about how they worked. Very early in life, young boys were encouraged to play hunting games with other little boys. They would practice shooting play bows and arrows, shooting small straw animals that their fathers made and tossed into the air. Until they were eight or nine, they might even play elaborate games of "house" with girls. The young girls would make small huts and pretend to send the boys out to hunt. The boys would come back with some morsel they had gotten from their mothers and would then act out typical adult behaviors. Boys would pretend to return from hunts, and girls would dance in celebration as they had seen their mothers and grandmothers do.

Although little Jean-Baptiste's young life was not typical, Sacagawea probably told him the same stories and sung him lullabies just as she would have back in the village. In the evenings at camp, she probably had help from the other members of the expedition. As the little infant turned into a toddler, the men would probably have taken turns bouncing him on their knees and encouraging him to dance to the fiddle, which two of the men liked to play. Apparently, Jean-Baptiste enjoyed music and often danced to the fiddle since he gained the nickname Dancing Boy. In some ways, then, Jean-Baptiste had experiences that were similar to those of Mandan toddlers his age, who learned to dance around the fires back in the village.

Somehow, in spite of the challenges of the trail, Sacagawea managed to raise her infant son through his first two years as a happy and healthy little boy. As soon as they returned to the Mandans, he probably began to fit back into the normal childhood most boys experienced. Sacagawea would have begun using the training in agriculture she had likely received as a young girl. Hidatsa women learned not just to plant, grow, and harvest corn and other crops, but also to collect and preserve seeds, dry corn and squash for winter storage, and build drying, winnowing, and storage structures and tools. Sacagawea was likely a skilled agriculturalist by anyone's standards in the nineteenth century by the time she met Lewis and Clark.[13] She probably did not use these skills much in her short life, yet she experienced many things that no other Hidatsa, Mandan, or Shoshone woman ever would. Eventually, she would also become one of the most famous Native Americans in history.

## NOTES

1. John W. W. Mann, *Sacajawea's People: The Lemhi Shoshones and the Salmon River Country* (Lincoln: University of Nebraska Press, 2004), 11.

2. Sydney Lamb, "Linguistic Prehistory of the Great Basin," in *International Journal of American Linguistics* 24 (1956): 95–100.

3. Deward E. Walker Jr., "A Revisionist View of Julian Steward and the Great Basin Paradigm from the North," in *Julian Steward and the Great Basin: The Making of an Anthropologist,* ed. Richard O. Clemmer, Daniel Myers, and Mary Elizabeth Rudden (Salt Lake City: University of Utah Press, 1999), 61–73.

4. Robert H. Lowie, "The Northern Shoshone," in *Anthropological Papers of the American Museum of Natural History* (New York: Trustees of the American Museum of Natural History, 1909), 2:169–307.

5. Mann, *Sacajawea's People,* 177.

6. Virginia Cole Trenholm and Maurine Carley, *The Shoshonis: Sentinels of the Rockies* (Norman: University of Oklahoma Press, 1964), 11–12.

7. Theda Purdue, ed., *Sifters: Native American Women's Lives* (Chapel Hill: University of North Carolina Press, 2000), 3.

8. James Willard Schultz, *Bird Woman* (New York: Houghton Mifflin, 1918), 94–115.

9. Virginia Bergman Peters, *Women of the Earth Lodges: Tribal Life on the Plains* (New Haven: Archon Books, 1995), 107.

10. Bergman Peters, *Women of the Earth Lodges*, 147–49.

11. Frank Henderson Stewart, "Hidatsa," in *Handbook of North American Indians* (Washington, D.C.: Smithsonian Institution, 2001), 13:334–35.

12. Robert H. Lowie, "Notes on the Social Organization and Customs of the Mandan, Hidatsa, and Crow Indians," in *Anthropological Papers of the American Museum of Natural History* (New York: Trustees of the American Museum of Natural History, 1917), 21:46.

13. Gilbert L. Wilson, *Buffalo Bird Woman's Garden: Agriculture of the Hidatsa Indians* (1917; repr. St. Paul: Minnesota Historical Society, 1987).

# Chapter 2

# TOUSSAINT CHARBONNEAU

Although people do not often remember the name of Sacagawea's husband, Toussaint Charbonneau was in fact the person hired as an interpreter for the Lewis and Clark expedition. Sacagawea came along as a bonus, since she could speak Shoshone. So who was this French trader turned interpreter and field guide for American expeditions? There is more recorded about his life than his wife's, and he lived longer. As far as can be determined, Toussaint Charbonneau was born around 1759 near Montreal. As an adult, he became a fur trader and lived among the Hidatsas and Mandans sometime in the late 1790s. Although the date of his death is also uncertain, there are records of his working as a trader and interpreter until sometime between 1839 and 1843. Unlike his young Shoshone wife, Sacagawea, who only lived until her early twenties, Charbonneau was likely in his late seventies or early eighties when he died.

## THE FRENCH FUR TRADE

When the French first came to North America in the early 1500s, they were hoping to find a way to profit from the new continent as the Spanish had done in Central and South America. Very early on in the French exploration of the Hudson Bay area of what is now Canada, the French perceived that furs could be a very profitable business. Soon, a brisk trade developed between the native peoples and the French throughout the north and eventually the northwest. American Indians trapped and prepared the furs of beaver, otter, fox, martens, and minks and traded them for knives, metal pots, mirrors, beads, guns, and ammunition. It quickly became a mutually desirable trade, and beaver furs in particular became very popular in Europe. As demand increased, prices also rose, making fur trading a very profitable enterprise.

In 1608, the explorer Samuel de Champlain founded a trading post that would eventually grow into the town of Quebec. As the fur trade expanded, organized companies took over control and organized the trade, making very large profits. The major fur-trading company, the Hudson Bay Company, was founded in 1670 by the English and employed many French traders. By this time, beaver pelts were in very high demand in Europe because they were used to make the very popular felt hats that most men wore. Furs of all kinds were also used in trimming coats for both men and women, and for lining gloves.

Eventually, the French and English would become competitors in the lucrative fur trade of North America. As the English created a string of permanent settlements along the Atlantic coastline of North America, the French pushed down from Quebec along the Mississippi River and competed for territory and trade with the Native Americans. Throughout the 1600s and the early 1700s, both sides argued over what was rightfully theirs to control, settle, and trade. In 1754, war broke out between France and England, partly over European issues and mostly over the contest for North America. At the end of this French and Indian War (or Seven Years' War as it was known in Europe), the French lost and Britain took over all North American territories. The French already in Canada remained as British subjects, and many of them continued to participate in the fur trade.

In the late 1700s, another fur-trading company was founded to compete with the dominant Hudson Bay Company. Called the North West Company, this enterprise pushed much farther west and traded with the Mandans, Hidatsas, and other people in the region. Although they were competitors, the two groups eventually merged in 1821. Between them, they controlled over 90 percent of the North American fur trade during the late 1700s and early 1800s. Eventually, American fur traders joined the British companies, especially after the Lewis and Clark expedition. Some of these American fur traders, known as "mountain men," trapped their own furs in the Rocky Mountain region. The American fur trade, however, did not survive much past the mid-1800s. By the 1830s, sales dropped drastically in Europe as felt hats went out of fashion, replaced by silk ones. Overhunting also led to a severe depopulation of beaver and other animals, making it harder and harder to find them. As the fur trade decreased, more and more permanent settlers moved into the West, creating an entirely new economic system.

As far as Mandan and Hidatsa participation in the trade is concerned, they were more like central brokers to the trade. Beavers were rare along the Knife River, and although the Mandans and Hidatsas had some buffalo furs, those did not fetch much of a price. Thus, the Mandans and Hidatsas became the chief suppliers of horses to Canadian fur traders and sold the guns and other goods they purchased from traders to other American Indian villages.[1] They also traded corn and other food products to both fur traders and other American Indians in exchange for metal pots, hoes, axes, knives, and other materials such as beads and cloth.

## FRENCH AND INDIAN MARRIAGES

Although most of the English settlers in North America remained along the coast and created towns that were clearly separated from native populations, French settlers had always developed a closer relationship with the American Indians. British settlement was motivated by financial profit, but also by the desire to acquire and own land, recreating English society in a new place. The French mostly saw the exploration and settlement of North America as an economic enterprise. Since most of the French settlers came without families, they often took wives among the native peoples they came to know and understand. In fact, American Indian women became very valuable members of the fur trade. They taught traders language, interpreted for them, and created kinship bonds that helped the French traders manage life in a new place.

American Indian women often were very willing to marry these French traders for various reasons. One factor was the gender imbalance in some tribes. Due to warfare, there were often fewer men than women, making it harder for Native American women to find husbands in their tribes. Some women became second or third wives of the same man, but many preferred to marry a French trader instead. Such a union also gave the woman access to goods she might not otherwise be able to afford. American Indian parents often encouraged their daughters to marry French traders for this reason or to guarantee an ongoing trading partnership.

Although the French sent Jesuit missionaries to convert the Indians, the French generally accepted the fact that native culture would not become more like European culture after conversion. Because of this tolerant attitude, the Indians were much more willing to create lasting relationships with the French than they were with the English, who demanded that the American Indians abandon their native culture after conversion. Although neither the English nor French gained many converts to

Christianity, the French had more success and a better overall relation-ship with the Indians. Thus, while the English stayed away from unions with "savages" and "heathens," the French found intermarriage with In-dians a good thing.

French marriage customs back in the motherland were similar to those in England. For a marriage to take place, both parents needed to consent to the marriage, since it tied the families together and could influence the economic and social status of both. It was also important in France that both husband and wife be Catholic and be married by a member of the clergy. In North America, however, some of these tradi-tions fell by the wayside. First, there were no French parents to provide consent, so traders were able to make their choices free from interfer-ence from at least that side. Secondly, since most American Indians did not convert to Christianity, a Catholic priest could not conduct the marriage ceremony. Thus, marriages between French traders and Indian women became "valid" by mutual consent. These mutual consent mar-riages became known as *la facon du pays* which meant "the custom of the country." For short, they were called "country marriages."[2] Sometimes a French trader had a "country wife" out on his trading circuit and an-other official wife back in whatever city or town he might call home. Most often, however, French traders came to North America as single men and had one or a series of Indian wives.

Indian marriages were traditionally ones in which the parents and the daughter or son consented to the union. Thus, American Indian women rarely felt forced into an undesirable marriage, and most marriages to French traders were ones that both the Indian woman and her family saw as beneficial. French traders might participate in a ceremony in which the family and clan of the woman gave gifts and received gifts. Mutual exchange of gifts cemented a bond of reciprocity between the families of the married couple. Although English observers would sometimes misin-terpret these exchanges as purchasing a bride, American Indian parents understood the union in a very different way. Most Indian wives of French traders were not considered sold slaves.

Sacagawea, however, was a captive when she married Toussaint Char-bonneau. It is possible that she had little choice in the marriage, or that she chose it as preferable to her previous position. It is also possible, however, that she was treated like an adopted daughter and that an exchange of gifts cemented the marriage as it was done traditionally. Some English observers might have seen this exchange as buying a wife or receiving her as win-nings in a gambling game. However, it may simply have been the Hidatsa marriage tradition of exchanging gifts in order to cement a marriage. There are no records or eyewitness accounts to tell us more about the marriage between Charbonneau and Sacagawea.

## TOUSSAINT CHARBONNEAU
## AS INTERPRETER

Many French settlers became permanent residents of American Indian tribes, and it appears that Toussaint Charbonneau lived with the Mandans and Hidatsas from the late 1790s perhaps until his death in the late 1830s or early 1840s. Such men fathered mixed-race, or Métis, children who grew up as completely accepted members of native clans and tribes. In some areas, a large Métis population developed from these unions between French traders and Indian women. Toussaint Charbonneau fathered at least two such children and perhaps more. Although he called the Mandan and Hidatsa villages along the Knife River his home, he spent a good portion of his adult life traveling, as most traders did.[3]

When Lewis and Clark arrived at the Mandan village in November of 1804, Charbonneau was in his mid-forties and would be the oldest member of the Corps of Discovery. He grew up near what became the city of Montreal and worked as a laborer for the North West Company as a young man. Part of his job was to carry various trade goods, like knives and tobacco, to American Indian camps. Eventually, he must have decided that he could do better on his own as a free trader and began trading among the Mandan villages by the late 1790s. He purchased trade goods from the trading company posts, took them to Indian villages, and obtained furs in payment. In order to make this trade work, Charbonneau and others like him, called "residenters," lived with the Indians and learned their ways. It was also necessary to gain the favor of various chiefs in order to keep the trade going, so living with the tribes helped establish good relationships.[4]

Charbonneau had two Indian wives when he met Lewis and Clark. It is not clear whether Sacagawea was the first or second wife, or even if she was a favorite. It is also not clear what kind of a relationship he had with his wives. Some scholars have accused Charbonneau of being a very cruel and brutal husband. There really is only one piece of evidence, a sentence in the Lewis and Clark journals where William Clark wrote, "I checked our interpreter for striking his woman at their Dinner."[5] Unfortunately, it was common for men to hit women in the nineteenth century but became less tolerated toward the end of the century. There is no other evidence that Charbonneau was a cruel man, although it is of course possible.

It does appear that he married many women during the course of his long life. None of these women left behind any records about what kind of a husband he was. However, we do know more about other aspects of his life. Much of this information comes from the Lewis and Clark journals. Apparently, Meriwether Lewis did not think very highly of Charbonneau. Often in his journals, Lewis wrote negatively about their French interpreter, at one point calling him "perhaps the most timid waterman in the world."[6] He could not swim and often appeared shaken when they encountered rough waters. On one occasion, a rainstorm brought a roaring flood down the river, requiring Clark, Charbonneau, and Sacagawea to scramble up a steep bank to avoid being washed away. Clark recorded that Charbonneau was "much Scared and nearly without motion" until Clark managed to persuade him to keep climbing up.[7] Charbonneau was no river man.

He was, however, a good cook. Having had to prepare his own food on many trading ventures, Charbonneau had learned to work with limited variety and prepare wild game with great skill. Soon, Charbonneau was cooking for the Corps of Discovery most of the time. One of his specialties was sausage made from buffalo meat. Even the critical Lewis called this sausage "one of the greatest delicacies of the forest."[8] He described the process in detail—how Charbonneau would mix some of the shoulder meat with suet and then stuff it into the emptied intestines of the buffalo and fry it in oil. This sausage was a very common and much desired meal for mountain men and traders when they had buffalo or similar game.[9]

After the Lewis and Clark expedition, Charbonneau kept cooking for various trading groups or his friends. One trader wrote in his journal in the mid-1830s about a Christmas meal that Charbonneau prepared for a group of people. Even as an old man probably in his mid-seventies, Charbonneau stirred up a meal of "meat pies, bread, fricasseed pheasants, boiled tongue, roast beef, and coffee."[10] This same trader, a man named Francis Chardon, mentioned Charbonneau's good food on a number of occasions in his journal. Apparently, Charbonneau could have been a successful chef if he had left the woods for cities and towns back east.

Certainly, Toussaint Charbonneau was a good interpreter. He had provided such services before the Lewis and Clark expedition and for most of the rest of his life. At times, he worked for the U.S. government as an interpreter, providing translation services to visiting dignitaries, artists, and others going west toward the Mandan and Hidatsa lands. In spite of his skill, however, he developed a reputation as difficult and unlikable through the work of writers of both fiction and nonfiction. Since he married many wives over the years, authors often portray him as a womanizer at best. Others describe him as an angry man with a gambling problem. Some contemporaries accused him of stirring up trouble between whites and Indians, but in spite of such an accusation, Charbonneau appears to have found steady work throughout most of his life. He was appreciated and paid very well for his work as an interpreter.[11]

Once the expedition was over, Lewis called him "a man of no peculiar merit" but that he had done well as an interpreter.[12] Lewis frequently referred to Charbonneau in his journals as irritating, careless at times, and more of a liability than an asset. Once, when they were negotiating for horses from the Shoshones, Charbonneau informed Lewis of an important decision the chiefs had made several hours afterward. Lewis believed that Charbonneau might have almost cost them the ability to continue the journey through simple carelessness. If he had not been a good cook, Lewis might not have tolerated him at all. Since Lewis needed Sacagawea, he decided to put up with Charbonneau on the journey. Lewis knew the expedition would need to purchase horses from the Shoshones, so Sacagawea's interpreting skills were vital to his success.

Clark, however, must have viewed Charbonneau as a valuable asset and even as a friend. After the expedition, Clark invited the interpreter to come with Sacagawea and their son to live with him in St. Louis. He offered to give Charbonneau a piece of land so that he could farm, and offered to adopt little Jean-Baptiste of whom he had become very fond.[13] Although some of his dedication to the child was undoubtedly out of loyalty and care for Sacagawea, it does seem that Clark saw Charbonneau as his friend. Many times in his journals, Clark wrote of walking along the riverbanks with both Sacagawea and her husband. He found their companionship agreeable and was constantly asking questions about the flora, fauna, and the native peoples of the region. Charbonneau's knowledge of the land from his travels as a trader must have been a great asset to Clark.

Although there is not much evidence concerning the relationship between Charbonneau and Sacagawea, the Lewis and Clark journals do speak of Charbonneau's participation in taking care of Sacagawea when she became deathly ill on the journey. While Lewis became very annoyed that Charbonneau had not forced Sacagawea to obey Lewis's strict dietary orders for her, Charbonneau did help feed her food and medicine when she was refusing them. Even though he could not steer a boat or demonstrate great bravery in times of danger, he did manage to keep up with all the others on the expedition, all of whom were younger and more experienced as river men.

Toussaint Charbonneau remains somewhat of a mystery, but he certainly made an impression on those he met in life. It was his wife, however, who would become the famous figure of the Lewis and Clark expedition.

# NOTES

1. W. Raymond Wood and Thomas D. Thiessen, *Early Fur Trade on the Northern Plains: Canadian Traders Among the Mandan and Hidatsa Indians, 1738–1818* (Norman: University of Oklahoma Press, 1985), 63.

2. Patrick Jung, "The Creation of Métis Society: French-Indian Intermarriage in the Upper Great Lakes," *Voyageur* (Winter/Spring 2003): 43.

3. Wood and Thiessen, *Early Fur Trade on the Northern Plains*, 46–47.

4. W. Dale Nelson, *Interpreters with Lewis and Clark: The Story of Sacagawea and Toussaint Charbonneau* (Denton: University of North Texas Press, 2003), 13.

5. William Clark, August 14, 1805, in *The Journals of the Lewis and Clark Expedition*, ed. Gary E. Moulton (Lincoln: University of Nebraska Press, 1983–2001). Also made available online by University of Nebraska Press at http://lewisandclarkjournals.unl.edu/index.html. Listed hereafter as *JLC*.

6. Meriwether Lewis, May 14, 1805, *JLC*.

7. Clark, June 29, 1805, *JLC*.

8. Lewis, May 9, 1805, *JLC*.

9. Nelson, *Interpreters with Lewis and Clark*, 27.

10. Ibid., 98.

11. Larry E. Morris, *The Fate of the Corps: What Became of the Lewis and Clark Explorers after the Expedition* (New Haven: Yale University Press, 2004), 133–34.

12. Donald Jackson, ed., *Letters of the Lewis and Clark Expedition with Related Documents, 1783–1854* (Urbana: University of Illinois Press, 1978), 1:368–69.

13. Nelson, *Interpreters with Lewis and Clark*, 66.

# Chapter 3

# JOINING THE EXPEDITION

Why did President Thomas Jefferson send an expedition into the northwest at the turn of the nineteenth century? What was the meaning of this journey that would make a young American Indian girl famous? A two-year project, this expedition would become an important event in the history of the United States, as well as in the lives of all the native peoples the Corps of Discovery met along the way.

## JEFFERSON'S DREAM

When Thomas Jefferson became the third president of the United States in 1801, he inherited a number of interesting issues, including ongoing efforts to prove the young nation was viable and strong. Key to the future of America's strength, Jefferson believed, was its large tracts of land. In fact, Jefferson often spoke of his hope that the United States would never become bogged down in labor and commercial issues as Britain frequently experienced. He believed that America could avoid European problems by remaining an agrarian paradise full of independent farmers. Sometimes referred to as the agrarian myth, Jefferson's vision of America was one of self-reliant producers of agricultural products and raw materials for export. This would help avoid the urban crowding and pollution of the early Industrial Revolution already underway in Britain and other parts of Europe.[1]

Even before Jefferson became president, he was interested in the West. This vast expanse of unexplored land could provide unknown resources for the young country, not the least of which was land for an increasing population. Plentiful land was central to his hopes for an America of independent farmers and artisans. Beyond this interest were many others. Jefferson had long been known as one of the preeminent members of the Enlightenment—an intellectual movement begun in the salons of Paris by those interested in science, discovery, politics, and a host of other subjects. Enlightenment thinkers ranged broadly in their interests, but at the basis of the movement was a desire to apply the new scientific ways of thinking to society. During the scientific revolution of the previous century, people like Isaac Newton and Galileo began to speak of observable laws that governed the motion of planets. Enlightenment philosophers began arguing during the 1700s that if there were observable laws governing nature, then perhaps there were similar observable laws governing society.[2]

Jefferson's participation in the Enlightenment movement shaped his thinking about the largely unknown American West. As had scientists and philosophers in Europe, Jefferson wanted to examine the West—to see what was out there. He wanted to know about the geology and geography of the region, to be sure. Some have argued that the Lewis and Clark expedition was all about finding the fabled Northwest Passage—a water route that was supposed to transect the North American continent all the way to the Pacific. Such a water route would enable rapid transport to the Pacific and thus better access to trade with China and the rest of the East. Europeans had been seeking faster routes to the East ever since Marco Polo's accounts of eastern riches reached Italy in 1269 C.E. Although explorers like Vasco de Gama and Bartolemew Diaz had explored routes for Europeans around Africa to the East, many early settlers of the Americas thought they could find a fast water route by going west. Although Christopher Columbus had bumped into large continents on his way west, later settlers to the Americas continued to hope for and search for a water route through to the Pacific.

By Jefferson's time, however, no one really believed there was a fast water route cutting through North America. Yet Jefferson did hope that the Missouri River could provide a good path toward the Rocky Mountains, and after a short portage over the mountains, another large river might complete the journey to the Pacific. Therefore, although Jefferson was under no illusions that his group of explorers would find a clear and easy "northwest passage," he did have hopes for an easy navigation route to the Pacific. This route would be important, not just for trade, but to make sure that Americans, rather than the British or Spanish, were able to settle the West.

This scientific-minded president also hoped to amass geological and botanical knowledge about the West and hoped that any expedition sent would collect specimens for later study. Additionally, Jefferson was very interested in the native peoples who lived in the West. He wanted to know more about them, study their lives and ways, and make contact with them to try to ensure that trade with those peoples would be with the United States exclusively. An expedition to the West, then, would seek to establish trade relations and secure the loyalty of these indigenous groups. He also hoped that the more information he gleaned about American Indians in the West, the better chances the United States would have of creating cooperative relationships between them and incoming white settlers. Thus, he hoped to avoid some of the strains and warfare that had occurred in the east as white settlers kept pushing west into native territories.

Interestingly, Thomas Jefferson had been investigating the possibility of a western expedition long before he became president. As early as 1783, while Jefferson was serving as a member of Congress, he looked into a possible expedition that would be privately funded. He tried to persuade George Rogers Clark, a hero of the American Revolution, which had only recently ended, to lead such an expedition. George Rogers Clark turned down the offer, and nothing came of these plans for a time. It would be his younger brother William Clark who would later be part of the expedition.[3] When Jefferson went to France as the American ambassador a few years later, he again tried to persuade someone to lead a western expedition. In 1792, when Jefferson was back in the United States and serving as secretary of state for George Washington, he tried to persuade an intellectual named Moses Marshall to lead a journey west. Marshall was a medical doctor and a botanist, a perfect scientist for such an expedition in Jefferson's judgment. Apparently, Marshall also turned him down.[4]

In 1793, Jefferson tried again with a French botanist named André Michaux. This time, the effort was one sponsored by the American Philosophical Society—the premier scientific organization in America at that time. Michaux actually made a start but apparently never made it west of the Mississippi River. At this point, other interests kept Jefferson from making any more attempts to sponsor a western expedition until he became president in 1801. However, others had made some of their own explorations, which provided more knowledge for Lewis and Clark. In 1792, a captain named Robert Gray, who traded up and down the Pacific coast of North America, found and named the Columbia River. This river is what Jefferson later hoped would be easy to portage to from the Missouri. Another seaman, British captain George Vancouver, made detailed maps of the Pacific coast and sent someone about 100 miles up the Columbia River for his surveys. At about this same time, fur traders sponsored by the Spanish went up the Missouri River and reached the Mandan villages where Lewis and Clark eventually met Sacagawea. One of these traders, John Thomas Evans, made excellent maps of the Missouri route to the Mandan villages, which Lewis and Clark later used for the first part of their journey.

Just as Jefferson became president, a book was published that convinced Jefferson he needed to make a western expedition finally happen. Alexander Mackenzie, an investor in the North West Company of Canada, wrote a description of a trip he took to the Arctic Ocean in 1789 and a later trip west across the Rockies to the Pacific coast of Canada. Called *Voyages from Montreal . . . through the Continent of North America, to the Frozen and Pacific Oceans*, Mackenzie's account inspired Jefferson.[5] If the United States did not sponsor its own expedition soon, others might lay claim to the land and prevent the young country from expanding. When the Spanish transferred western territories to the French as part of a peace settlement to Napoleon in 1800, he had plans to use the land as a colony. However, he soon realized how difficult it would be to maintain control of such a far-flung region, especially with so many competing powers in the region. Napoleon then offered to sell "Louisiana" to the United States in 1803, and Jefferson jumped at the offer. This made the western expedition even easier to accomplish. Jefferson would now add to the expedition's goals that of asserting sovereignty over the newly acquired region.[6]

## THE CORPS OF DISCOVERY

With all these goals in mind, Jefferson finally selected Meriwether Lewis to lead the expedition west. Lewis was a Virginian, like Jefferson, and grew up on a large plantation only about 10 miles away from Monticello, Jefferson's home. Lewis's father had served in the Continental army during the Revolutionary War, so Lewis followed his father's example and joined the army as a young man in 1794. He served along the frontier and rose in the ranks to captain by 1800. In 1801, Jefferson appointed Lewis his personal secretary and began talking to him about a western expedition. Lewis was, in Jefferson's opinion, the best man to lead. He was a strong man with excellent conditioning from his time in the army.

As Lewis began preparing himself for the western expedition, he realized he would need a coleader to meet the growing list of goals. William Clark, whom both Lewis and Jefferson knew, became this man. Clark grew up in Louisville, Kentucky, and joined the Kentucky militia at age 19. Eventually, he joined the regular army and reached the rank of captain by 1795. Lewis served under Clark for a time and began what would become a lasting friendship. Clark became the map maker of the expedition, recording compass readings, measurements of distances, and other important data. Although his journal entries would be rougher than Lewis's and filled with grammatical errors, he often seemed to have more to say and recorded his thoughts about the native peoples they encountered along the way.

Most of what we know about the expedition, including Sacagawea, comes from Lewis and Clark's journals. A few other men, however, left behind journals that sometimes add interesting perspectives. The other writers included Sergeants Patrick Gass and John Ordway and Private Joseph Whitehouse. These three men wrote much shorter entries than did Lewis and Clark, but they recorded almost every day with some details about their tasks. Clark wrote on a consistent basis and made many observations about the country and Native American cultures. By far, however, Lewis kept the most detailed records, including distances covered, weather conditions for each day of each month, and other astronomical observations about moon phases. Because of his extensive writing, one must rely heavily on Lewis's version of events. It is amazing that anyone other than Lewis and Clark took the time to write almost daily journals.

Eventually, the expedition would include 31 permanent members. Besides Lewis and Clark, there were 4 sergeants and 24 privates. There were 7 nonmilitary members of the group, including Toussaint Charbonneau, Sacagawea, their child (Jean-Baptiste), and the Negro slave York. There was one additional member of the Corps—Seaman, Lewis's Newfoundland dog. Although his color never appears in the journals, tradition says he was black. We do know that Lewis was very proud of his canine companion and frequently mentions him in his journals. Seaman caught squirrels and other small animals that the group used as food. He also served as guard, barking an alarm when a buffalo swam across the river close to one of the riverboats or when bears came into camp looking for food.

One day, a wounded beaver bit Seaman, severing an artery that Lewis struggled hard to stanch. Although Lewis feared the dog would die, Seaman recovered and was soon busy barking warnings and fetching small game. Once he even managed to catch a wounded deer that had run into the river. Seaman caught the deer, drowned it, and then dragged it back to shore, demonstrating his excellent swimming skills. There are other journal entries about the dog's encounter with sharp barbs that hurt his feet. Another entry talks about how the Lemhi Shoshones were very impressed with the dog and wanted to buy him from Lewis. He records that no price would be enough to persuade him to sell Seaman.[7]

Besides the permanent members, there were others who would only travel as far as the Mandan villages and then return to St. Louis with reports. These 10 or so men would be able to give a progress report to Jefferson after the first leg of the journey. The entire group left St. Louis in mid-May 1804 and reached the Mandan villages in late October. The return party then headed back to St. Louis in the spring of 1805, while the permanent party, along with Sacagawea and her husband and son, headed west.

Originally, captains Lewis and Clark named the expedition the "Corps of Volunteers on an Expedition of North Western Discovery." This title is the only one referred to by any of the expedition members until Sergeant Patrick Gass published his journal of the trip in 1807. In his journal, he called the group the "Corps of Discovery," which has since become the popular designation.[8] This group, whatever they called themselves at the time, was finally prepared for the trip and ready to head up the Missouri River with their barge or keelboat and two pirogues (large rowboats) in the spring of 1805.

The first part of the trip was not particularly difficult, and the spirits of the corps members must have been high as they started north. Soon, the summer heat became the greatest enemy, and the men struggled with heat exhaustion and fatigue. They made good progress, however, averaging 15 miles a day through relatively quiet and easy-to-navigate waters. They met a variety of friendly American Indians along the way and held councils with such groups as the Otos and Missouris, handing out peace medals to the important leaders. The corps did suffer its only casualty of the trip—Sergeant Charles Floyd died of what was likely a burst appendix. They buried him along the river near the present site of Sioux City, Iowa.

## WITH THE MANDANS

By October, the corps had reached the Mandan and Hidatsa villages where they would spend the winter. It was here that Sacagawea and her husband and child joined the Corps of Discovery. The expedition began building winter quarters outside of the villages and traded with the locals for food and other necessary supplies to get them through the winter. For five months, the corps began to learn about native culture, as the native peoples in turn learned about the white man. At first, Lewis and Clark were optimistic that they could forge a good alliance among a number of tribes in the region, including the Mandans, Hidatsas, and Arikaras. Their plan was to convince these peoples to agree to peaceful coexistence and trade with future American merchants from St. Louis, instead of trading with the Sioux and the British traders from the north.

At one point in the winter, Lewis and Clark were so intent on demonstrating their loyalty as allies that they suited up for battle with the Sioux after they heard about the actions of a Sioux raiding party. Although the Mandans were impressed, they also must have chuckled to themselves while calmly explaining to the white men that revenge could be sought in the spring, when traveling would not be so dangerous. They were used to raids from other tribes, who expected revenge raids in return. In spite of long efforts and perhaps even good intentions, Lewis and Clark did not manage to create any long-lasting alliances among the native peoples. Once the expedition headed west, relationships among the tribes continued much as they always had.

The winter was, however, an excellent time of visiting, dancing, and celebrating together, and of survival. Most efforts were spent hunting for food and trading with the Mandans for corn, meat, and other supplies. In return, the Mandans were happy to receive trade goods, particularly metal objects such as axes, hoes, and pots. Often, trade objects were not used the way their makers had intended. For example, someone in the corps gave a small corn-grinding mill to one of the Mandans. The new owner took it apart and used at least one portion of metal as part of "a pounder for making grease from buffalo marrow bones."[9] Indians would come to the fort to have hoes and axes repaired, and to trade for other metal goods if possible. Toward the end of the winter, the expedition began smithing war axes out of whatever scrap metal was available, since such axes were very popular. This constant flow of new objects ensured the corps a steady supply of corn and meat.

Sacagawea and Toussaint Charbonneau entered this interesting life in Fort Mandan in early November. Clark's journal mentions Charbonneau visiting the fort and offering his services as an interpreter to the expedition. The corps had used a variety of interpreters along their journey so far, but the prospect of employing one full-time for the rest of the expedition was a happy one for Clark. Charbonneau also offered to bring his two wives along on the journey. He told Clark that since they were both "Snake Indians," they could also serve as interpreters. Lewis and Clark decided to hire Charbonneau, but wanted to bring only one of his wives along on the journey.

There is no way of knowing why Sacagawea was the wife chosen for the expedition. Perhaps she was the favorite of the two wives, or perhaps she was tougher and therefore better able to make the journey. However, the irony is that Sacagawea was pregnant when Lewis and Clark first met her and would give birth to Jean-Baptiste before the group left in the spring. Bringing Sacagawea on the trip meant also bringing along a

newborn baby. For whatever reason, Lewis and Clark agreed to this arrangement, and Sacagawea was the chosen wife for the journey. The men
in Fort Mandan made little mention of her in their diaries that winter.
At one point, Sergeant John Ordway wrote that a "frenchmans Squaw
came to our camp who belonged to the Snake nation. She came with
our interpreter's wife and brought with them 4 buffalow robes and gave
them to our officers."[10] It is not clear that either of these women were
Sacagawea, but one might have been. Again, on Christmas, Sergeant
Patrick Gass wrote in his journal that the interpreter and his wives joined
in the celebrations in the fort. He mourns the fact that they were the only
women around for the festivities.[11]

Another journal reference in January reveals that one of the interpreter's wives was sick, but there are no further mentions, and there is no
way to know if it was Sacagawea. At this point, she would have been
about eight months pregnant. Later in the spring when the expedition
was in full swing preparing for the rest of their journey, Clark wrote that
he planned to take an interpreter and his two Indian wives on the journey.
Perhaps he had changed his mind about bringing only one of the wives;
however, when the expedition headed out later, only Sacagawea accompanied her husband.

On April 7, 1805, Lewis and Clark sent the keelboat back to St. Louis
with a crew of men they no longer needed for their journey. They also
sent back maps, specimens, and other scientific information gathered the
previous summer and fall. Among the treasures were several birds and a
live prairie dog that they found to be a very interesting creature. With the
other members safely sent back south, Lewis, Clark, and the rest of the
group made their own departure. It must have taken a large measure of
courage for a young mother to take her baby into the unknown. She carried Jean-Baptiste on her back in a cradle board like all the other Mandan
mothers did, and she brought along some baby clothes and blankets for
her child.

In most of the journal records of the journey, Sacagawea was referred
to as "the interpreter's wife" or "the interpreter's squaw." It must have
been difficult to learn to pronounce her name or know how to spell it. In
Clark's journal entry on the departure day (April 7, 1805), he painstak-
ingly spells out "Sah-kah-gar-we-a."[12] Some readers of the journal think
this name might have been added later. This notation is really the only
time any of the expedition members write out Sacagawea's proper name.
The brave, young mother would thus be known as "wife" or "squaw" until
much later when historians and novelists began to write about her nearly
100 years after the famous trip.

## THE JOURNEY BEGINS

The journey west began as a convoy of six dugout canoes and two pirogues, larger boats that would carry most of the equipment and supplies for the trip. Sacagawea and her new baby, Jean-Baptiste, would ride in one of these larger boats with her husband, Toussaint, and others. Imagine managing the care of a young baby under such conditions. Sacagawea had to feed her baby every few hours, clean and wash the child, and keep him either sleeping or contented while awake, bouncing along the waves of the Missouri River. One of the interesting absences in the journals of the expedition is any real mention of a crying or unhappy baby. Apparently, Sacagawea did an excellent job of keeping baby Jean-Baptiste happy and contented on the journey.

One wonders, however, if it took a long time for Sacagawea to gain the respect of her companions. Since she was a wife of their interpreter, the men probably treated her kindly and respectfully. It is not clear, however, how these men might have viewed her. They knew that wives were often little more than slaves, purchased from American Indians as both laborers and companions. There is no clear mention of how Toussaint treated his wife, for the most part. Certainly, some of the men viewed Indian women as very loose and their men as very willing to sell nights with their wives to interested parties for the right price.

One of the men who kept a consistent journal during the expedition was Sergeant Patrick Gass. He had received very little education in his life, but his journal was later edited and embellished by a schoolmaster, who published it in 1807. In his entry on April 5 just before they headed west from the Mandan village, Gass wrote that he knew of a chief who had sold a night with his wife to a trader for a tobacco box.[13] It could be that this part was embellishment after the fact, but it does illustrate some of the views the men had of American Indian women and how their husbands treated them. In this context, one wonders how Sacagawea managed to relate to these men. Perhaps there were some difficult moments early in the journey, but there is no mention of such troubles in the journals.

Lewis and Clark had gathered information about the river and what lay ahead from the Mandans and Hidatsas before starting out that April. They expected the first part of the journey to go smoothly but were not sure what would happen when they had to cross the mountains that blocked them from further water routes. They hoped to find a short portage to the Columbia River but knew that they would need horses to make that part of the journey and were grateful to have Sacagawea along to help communicate with the Shoshones, who had those horses. Several peaceful days of rowing upriver passed, and all seemed well for the expedition.

After rowing in the boats during the day, Sacagawea, her baby, and husband shared a tent at night with Lewis and Clark. Lewis described the tent in his journals as one "made in the Indian stile [sic]" out of buffalo skins tied together with sinews.[14] It was a teepee, and somewhere in the boats, they carried with them the poles to stretch the skins over; they set this up every night and slept. It was probably fairly warm and dry, but not particularly ideal for a young wife and mother. Sacagawea must have sought to keep the newborn baby quiet in a tent filled with three men. She had no privacy or home of her own for the length of the journey.

In addition to interesting living conditions, the unpredictable spring weather also affected the journey. On the second day of the expedition, one of the boats filled with water and soaked one of the barrels of gunpowder and a bag of biscuit flour. They spread the flour out to dry in the sun in the hope of saving at least part of it. Right away, it became clear that Sacagawea's knowledge of native plants would be very helpful to the expedition. The next day, Lewis wrote in his journal that Sacagawea "busied herself in serching [sic] for the wild artichokes which the mice collect and deposit in larger hoards."[15] She soon found a large amount of these roots buried in the ground. These were likely Jerusalem artichokes that grow plentifully in the region and were long cultivated by Native Americans. They are essentially sunflowers whose roots grow fat and taste much like potatoes when lightly boiled or steamed. This must have been a welcome addition to the foods that the expedition brought.

Most of the time, the Corps of Discovery relied on fresh game for meat and supplemented this meat with bread or biscuits baked from flour they brought with them. Any kind of fresh plant food came from Sacagawea's efforts along the way. The corps probably came to appreciate this contribution even more than her translation skills. Eventually, the corps ate dog meat they purchased from American Indians when no other game was available. Sacagawea did not become the cook for the expedition, but her supplements must have been viewed with great pleasure and anticipation as the weeks and months went by.

For most of the first month of the journey, life settled into a steady routine. The boats usually managed to make 15 to 20 miles each day, and Clark usually walked along the shore, observing the surrounding country. Apparently, he often took Sacagawea and her baby and husband along on his walks. It might have felt safer to Sacagawea to walk with her baby strapped to her back, especially when the wind was strong, as it often was. There were sails on the pirogues, which could help move these larger boats upstream, but they could sometimes prove dangerous. Seven days into the journey, the wind picked up suddenly that afternoon and nearly capsized one of the boats. Lewis wrote that evening in his journal that they had nearly lost the boat but managed to turn it just in time and lower the sail. That boat carried most of the scientific instruments and trade goods and usually carried Sacagawea and her baby. He wrote that they would likely have drowned had the boat capsized with them aboard.[16] Perhaps this event encouraged Sacagawea to join Clark on his almost daily walks along the shore.

Along the way, Sacagawea provided what information she knew about regional climates and the customs of the inhabitants. Private Joseph Whitehouse recorded in his journal on April 25 that Sacagawea told them the area they were passing through seldom received rain and never any dew.[17] A few days later, she brought Clark a bush that had berries that looked like cherries and tasted good. On another following day, she pointed out some pieces of red cloth left behind in an abandoned Indian camp they passed. Sacagawea explained that leaving bits of red cloth was a customary gift to the creator whenever the Indians left a summer or winter camp for different surroundings.[18]

As Sacagawea began habitually walking with Clark on the riverbank each day, she gathered food along the way. Two of the plants she found in the early journey were a type of wild licorice and a "white apple." While it is not clear what these white apples were, the wild licorice plant grows throughout the region of North Dakota and its roots were commonly used by Native Americans. Supplementing the expedition's diet with tubers provided their diet with much needed carbohydrates and sugars that a diet of primarily meat could not provide. Without Sacagawea's knowledge of regional plants, which she had learned as a child, the expedition might have even gone hungry.

She was yet to serve in any interpreting capacity, but already by the end of the first month of the journey, Sacagawea proved herself a vital part of the expedition and a ready source of information. Somehow, through all her food-gathering activity, she managed to care for and raise her young son. As she settled him down for the night in her tent with her husband and the two leaders of the corps, she must have thought about what might lie ahead and whether she would see her family again. Would they recognize her? Would she recognize them? Many years had now passed since she was a 12-year-old girl. She was now a wife, mother, and an important participant on an ambitious expedition led by the people who now claimed her land and called her people "children of the great white father."

# NOTES

1. Natalie S. Bober, *Thomas Jefferson: Draftsman of a Nation* (Charlottesville: University of Virginia Press, 2007).

2. Ira Owen Wade, *The Intellectual Origins of the French Enlightenment* (Princeton, NJ: Princeton University Press, 1971).

3. Kenneth C. Carstens and Nancy Son Carstens, eds., *The Life of George Rogers Clark, 1752–1818, Triumphs and Tragedies* (Westport, CT: Praeger, 2004).

4. James P. Ronda, *Thomas Jefferson and the Changing West* (St. Louis: Missouri Historical Society Press, 1997).

5. Alexander Mackenzie, *Voyages from Montreal on the River St. Laurence throughout the Continent of North America, to the Frozen and Pacific Oceans in the Years 1789 and 1793* (Ann Arbor, MI: University Microfilms, 1966).

6. Gary E. Moulton, ed., "Introduction," in *The Journals of the Lewis and Clark Expedition* (listed hereafter as *JLC*), footnote 9 of the online edition made available by University of Nebraska Press at http://lewisandclarkjournals.unl.edu/index.html.

7. http://www.lewisandclarktrail.com/newfoundland.htm.

8. http://www.pbs.org/lewisandclark/inside/wclar.html.

9. James P. Ronda, *Lewis & Clark among the Indians* (Lincoln: University of Nebraska Press, 1984), 104.

10. John Ordway, November 11, 1804, in *JLC*, ed. Gary E. Moulton (Lincoln: University of Nebraska Press, 1983–2001).

11. Patrick Gass, December 25, 1804, *JLC*.

12. William Clark, April 7, 1805, *JLC*.

13. Gass, April 5, 1805, *JLC*.

14. Meriwether Lewis, April 7, 1805, *JLC*.

15. Lewis, April 8, 1805, *JLC*.

16. Lewis, April 13, 1805, *JLC*.

17. Joseph Whitehouse, April 25, 1805, *JLC*.

18. Whitehouse, May 2, 1805, *JLC*.

# Chapter 4

# STRUGGLES ON THE JOURNEY

Not all of the journey went as smoothly as the first few weeks seemed to go. After all, this was wild country and very rough terrain. While the first part of the Missouri River from St. Louis to the Mandan villages had been fairly calm and easy to navigate, upstream became more and more swift and contained dangerous rocks, falls, and eddies. The most dangerous element, however, seemed to be the unpredictable weather.

## DANGERS OF THE RIVER

Part of the problem on the river was the spring wind. At times, sudden gusts would nearly capsize one of the pirogues, and at other times, the canoes had difficulty navigating the waves whipped up by the wind. Lewis often complained in his journals about the wind and the weather. It made progress difficult and the length of their journey uncertain. On May 14, 1805, what appeared to be a calm day suddenly turned stormy. In an unusual moment, both Lewis and Clark found themselves walking on the riverbank, helplessly watching as a sudden gust hit the river and nearly overturned the pirogue that contained most of the important equipment and supplies. For some reason, Charbonneau was in charge of steering the boat, something the corps seldom had him do. Instead of turning into the wind, he panicked and turned the boat against the wind, which leaned it completely over on its side.

Lewis wrote in his journal that Charbonneau "was perhaps the most timid waterman in the world."[1] Lewis and Clark recalled the event in their journals as a difficult one, but Lewis's writing revealed a level of anger and ridicule of Charbonneau and his lack of ability. The boat was eventually righted, but much of its contents were soaked. The hero of the day, however, was Charbonneau's wife, Sacagawea. She was in the boat when it began to capsize and instead of panicking as her husband did, she calmly went about trying to catch items that were falling out of the boat. Because of her calm efforts, many papers, instruments, books, medicines, and trading goods were saved from being washed down the river. Even though Lewis rarely wrote anything about Sacagawea, he did record with gratitude her efforts that day. Sacagawea was the calm one in a crisis, even with a baby on her back in a capsizing boat. If she had not already gained the admiration of the party, she did so that day.

To honor her perhaps for her bravery, the corps named a river in her honor about six days after the trouble on the water. This river or stream likely entered the Missouri somewhere near the present day Fort Peck Dam. It is not clear now where the stream actually was, and its name was soon changed to "Crooked Creek."[2] Although the name did not endure, this event illustrates how highly the Corps of Discovery thought of Sacagawea. She had done no interpreting yet, the primary reason she had been brought along. Her knowledge about the region and her cool head in a crisis were enough to make her a valuable member of the expedition.

Another problem that expedition members encountered on this part of the trip was various physical ailments. Lewis wrote one day that he had treated several men for boils and even more of them for sore eyes.[3] Later in their journey, they would encounter a good number of Indians who also had eye problems. Lewis later surmised that perhaps the sore eyes were caused by staring at the bright water reflecting and magnifying sunlight. It might have been some kind of reaction to insects that also harassed them. Being constantly on or beside water meant that they would have experienced a lot of trouble with mosquitoes.

Dangers of the river also included the constant erosion of the riverbank by the spring melts further west in the mountains. As the snow melted, the waters of the Missouri began to rise and often rush through tight areas. This rushing water weakened the mud riverbanks, causing occasional mud slides, some of them quite large. Lewis wrote about the mud slides and commented that they had barely missed being hit by one.[4] Apparently, these mud slides were big enough to have capsized the boats. Sacagawea must have been nervous about the safety of her young baby, but if she was, no one wrote about it in the journals.

So far, they had encountered no American Indians during the journey since leaving Fort Mandan. In late May, they passed some old camps, and Sacagawea studied the moccasins they found there, stating that the people were not Shoshone. Occasionally, the water washed a lodge pole down the river. There were signs that Indians had lived there, but there were no people. Some of these might have been summer camps that were not inhabited yet or possibly villages that had been devastated by outbreaks of smallpox. So far, the corps was able to find plenty of local game, so they did not need to rely on trade with Indians. Later in the expedition, this would not be the case.

Some of the game they found, however, was not always welcome. The men had heard stories about bears from the Mandans and Hidatsas and were happy to finally see some bears. Yet, the men remained cautious of these very strong and strange creatures. One of the men encountered a very large bear when out hunting and shot it. But, instead of dying, the bear turned on the hunter and began chasing him. William Bratton, the hunter, ran back to the riverbank and told Lewis about his encounter. Not wanting good bear meat to go to waste, Lewis and seven other men headed back into the woods to find the wounded bear.

Although they had expected to find the bear dead, they found it in some thick brush and shot it again, killing it this time. Lewis later wrote the following description of the encounter:

> We finally found him (the bear) concealed in some very thick brush and shot him through the skull . . . it was a monstrous beast . . . these bear being so hard to die rather intimidates us all; I must confess that I do not like the gentleman and had rather fight two Indians than one bear.[5]

There would be several more occasions when wounded bears would chase the hunters, making them run off without their guns and hatchets. The river was rapid, but so were the bears. The day after the above encounter, Lewis again wrote of bears:

> I walked on shore this morning for the benefit of exercise . . . in these excursions I most generally went alone armed with my rifle and espontoon [a spear-like weapon]; thus equipped I feel myself more than an equal match for a brown bear provided I get him in open woods or near the water . . . I have therefore come to a resolution to act on the defensive only, should I meet these gentlemen in the open country.[6]

Lewis's deep respect for bears is evident in both his caution and the habit he developed of calling them "gentlemen."

As the first weeks of the journey passed, the journal entries often mention rough weather. Some days were so windy that the expedition members were forced to wait until the following day to make forward progress.

When that happened, the men spent the day repairing equipment and hunting for food or sport. Since game was plentiful, they had enough to eat during this part of the trip, but the effort it took to battling currents and weather must have discouraged them at times. Yet there were often good days and always new things to see and marvel about. One day, the expedition saw a very large herd of buffalo and a wolf that was whiter than the wool on most sheep.[7] The amazement they felt at such sights is clear when reading the journals. The Corps of Discovery was indeed "discovering" a new and strange world with each step and paddle stroke.

Throughout the month of May, the journal writers record very cold mornings and often lots of ice frozen in the bottoms of the canoes. They had to bundle themselves with all their clothes, blankets, and skins that they might have collected. It rained almost every day and night, and one can imagine how miserable it must have been trying to sleep on soggy ground. Although they had tents to sleep in, they did not have floors that would protect them from the mud. Almost every morning now was spent drying out clothing and supplies. Lewis complained in his journal of being cold at night, and one wonders how Sacagawea managed to keep her baby warm and healthy during these cold nights. Eventually, however, she herself would succumb to an illness from which it seemed she might not recover.

## SICKNESS

For the first week or so of June, Lewis and Clark record raw, cold days with wind and intermittent rain. By the 10th, Sacagawea was very ill, although it is not clear what kind of illness she had or whether it was brought on by the bad weather. The day before, Lewis had complained in his journal of being unwell, and that he took some salts and felt much better. At various times on the journey, Lewis and Clark would treat ill members of the party for a variety of ailments. Most of the problems likely came from drinking bad water or spoiled meat. However, Sacagawea's illness seemed the worst of any, and for a while, both Lewis and Clark feared she might die.

In the journals, Lewis mentioned that Clark "bled her" as a treatment for her illness that first day. Bloodletting is a very old remedy for disease, first practiced by the ancient Egyptians and Mesopotamians. The Greeks studied the human body, and the famous doctor Galen discovered the circulation system in the second century c.e. He incorrectly assumed that illness could be caused by having too much blood in the veins, and that bleeding a patient would relieve pressure and disease in the body. Although this practice was first questioned as early as the sixteenth century, people still used the practice well into the nineteenth century. By the end of the 1800s, people came to recognize what most doctors then knew—that bloodletting did nothing for the body except possible harm.[8]

Although Sacagawea was still very ill, Clark bled her again the next night and recorded in his journal that it "appeared to be of great service to her."[9] Lewis, however, continued to have troubles and appeared to be suffering from dysentery or some kind of intestinal distress, probably from bad water. After taking salts the day before, he felt better the next day, but after a full day with a hunting party, he began to have symptoms again. He and the hunting party camped for the night, and since Lewis had no salts or medicines with him, he tried an old remedy he had learned from his mother. Apparently, Mrs. Lewis had a reputation in Virginia as an herb doctor and often used natural remedies to cure illness.[10] He made an herbal drink and seemed to cure himself of his ailment.

When Lewis returned to the rest of the corps the following day, he found Sacagawea feeling much worse and two other members of his party with physical ailments. Clark got out his medicines to treat one man with a boil on his hand and another with a toothache. While he did not record what he used to treat these problems, the common treatment for a toothache was to pull the tooth. Sometimes people used laudanum drops for the pain. Laudanum was a popular nineteenth-century drug—opium—used to treat almost every ache or pain. Clark wrote that he gave Sacagawea medicine that night, probably laudanum.

The concern of the entire expedition was now evident in the journals of all those who recorded the journey. On June 12, Private Joseph Whitehouse wrote:

> Our interpreters wife got very Sick, and great care was taken of her, knowing, what a great loss she would be, if she died, she being our only Interpreter, for the Snake Indians, who reside in those Mountains lying West of us, and from whom we expect assistance, in prosecuting our Voyage.[11]

The next day, Clark tried another dose of salts, while another member of the corps fell ill. Sacagawea's husband tried to persuade her to take more medicines, but she refused to do so. Lewis again wrote in his journal how worried he was about her. He also talked about how dependent the corps was on being able to trade for horses from Sacagawea's people once they arrived there.

Clark tried some bark poultices applied to her belly and thighs, and these seemed to help her. Lewis did the same the following day and made

her drink mineral water of some sort. Again, she refused medicines and
would only take them if her husband insisted. Clark wrote about how
frustrated he was and blamed Charbonneau for not taking better care of
his wife.[12] The concern of everyone was clear. Finally, after over a week
of very serious symptoms and no improvement, Sacagawea began to get
better. Lewis became frustrated at Charbonneau for letting her eat too
much too soon, and she once again took a turn for the worse. However,
by the end of another week, she seemed herself, and the entire Corps of
Discovery breathed a sigh of relief. Soon, she was collecting roots and
even fishing.

Lewis and Clark kept a watchful eye on their very important interpreter
and the health of the entire expedition. From time to time, one or another
of the team would fall ill, usually from drinking polluted water. Although
Sacagawea's ailment was unknown, most of the men who became sick
displayed symptoms of dysentery or some other kind of gastrointestinal
distress. Before the trip, they had procured the help of Dr. Benjamin Rush,
an interesting man who made his own medicines for various illnesses. He
provided packages of pills for the journey, and often the journals mention
"Rush's pills" used for first one person and then another. Most of the time,
these pills seemed to have the desired effect, although it is not clear what
the pills were actually made of.

Whenever they could, people in the eighteenth and nineteenth centuries drank mineral water, if they found natural springs. Spas sprung up
around such sources of water because people believed that bathing in the
water relieved everything from arthritis to rheumatism. They also drank
the water to treat internal digestive problems. Just as Sacagawea was recovering from her illness and the men were scouting along the riverbank
for a good place to portage around some falls, they found a mineral spring.
Apparently, the men drank quite a lot of the water when they found it,
which made them feel better right away. We can only surmise from the
following account by Whitehouse that many of the men suffered digestive
problems from the diet of wild game:

> opposite to which we found on the south side a beautiful sulfur
> or mineral spring running out of the side of the hills, the water
> having a strong sulfurous taste. Our party drank a considerable
> quantity of this water for their healths which had the desired
> effect.[13]

Lewis brought back some of the water for Sacagawea and made her drink
it. He believed that this water was instrumental in curing her illness.

Now that Sacagawea was well again, a very dangerous and difficult part of the journey began—an 18-mile-long portage around some falls and rapids on the river that the boats could not manage. Before beginning this difficult crossing, the party had to become engineers and carpenters, constructing wagons or carts to haul the canoes up and over the hilly terrain. They made axles out of the mast of one of the pirogues and then hid the boat in some trees with a cache of supplies they thought too heavy to take farther.[14] It took them 10 days to make the portage through difficult rocks, prickly pear cactus, and bad weather. On nearly the last day of the portage, a sudden storm arose just as Clark, Charbonneau, and Sacagawea were making the final leg of the journey. As the sudden rain poured down, a flash flood sent water and rock pouring down the hillside and into the valley.

Although they had taken shelter under a rock overhang, the flooding made it obvious that they would have to seek higher ground or be swept away in the river. The three tried to scramble up the rocky cliff face to higher ground, Clark pushing Sacagawea and the baby from behind, and Charbonneau pulling from above. Clark recorded in his journal that Charbonneau was very frightened, almost to the point of motionlessness, but somehow managed to help Clark drag Sacagawea and the baby to safety.[15] They managed to make the top of the hill just before more than 10 feet of water filled the ravine where they had been moments before. Clark lost his compass in the flood but later recovered it. Also lost, but not recovered, were most of baby Jean-Baptiste's clothing and blankets, as well as his father's gun.

Once the water had subsided and the portage was completed, Lewis began to assemble a strange, experimental boat or canoe. Anticipating more difficult portages and shallow waters ahead, he planned to abandon one or both of the pirogues and replace them with a boat made of a metal frame, covered with skins. He had the frame constructed before leaving St. Louis and hauled it along the journey up to this point. Over the past several weeks, he had employed various men sewing animal skins to cover the boat. When he finally put it together, he had no tar to waterproof it, so it began to leak. Although it might have been a very light and easy-to-portage vessel, it would not stay afloat, and Lewis had no choice but to abandon his experiment. Clark sent crews out to begin hollowing some new canoes.

Lewis had probably based his plans for the experimental boat on American Indian vessels. Many native peoples supplemented their dugout canoes with boats made from light wood frames covered with skins or bark. Some of these boats took the shape of a traditional canoe, and others a round bowl. The early kayaks of the northwestern natives were made from sealskins. All these boats had a long history of success, but key to all of them was a light wood frame and, more importantly, some kind of pitch to make the seams watertight. Lewis had brought along a kiln with which to burn pinewood to obtain tar, but he could not get it to work probably. Since Lewis lacked the proper pitch or tar, his experiment was doomed to failure.[16] Sacagawea had probably journeyed and fished in bark-covered boats herself and might have even assisted the Shoshone or Mandan women in preparing skins or bark for boat coverings. One wonders if she lent any advice to Lewis or simply shook her head at his efforts.

## QUIET CONTRIBUTIONS

As the weeks went by, Sacagawea returned to her usual work, gathering wild berries and roots to supplement the group's diet, caring for her infant son, and making observations about the countryside for Lewis and Clark when they were interested. Whenever they passed by signs of Indians, such as abandoned villages, Sacagawea investigated and told the Corps what she knew. It is clear from reading the journals of expedition members that Sacagawea was not serving as a guide on this trip. Although there were a few occasions when she did recognize the region of her childhood home and gave advice on what she saw there, she did not point out the way as many legends have implied. Just before she had fallen ill, Lewis wrote that they had arrived at a very large fork in the river. They were now faced with a dilemma—which fork to take as the main branch of the Missouri. If they made a mistake, it could mean weeks and even months of lost time, which might discourage the group from completing the journey. Therefore, Lewis sent men in canoes up both forks so he could make an informed choice, which he eventually did.[17]

Lewis began recording in his journal his surprise that they had not encountered any Indians yet, and that hoped they soon would. They were now moving out of buffalo country and were finding it harder to bring in meat, their primary food supply. On July 19, Sacagawea made some observations for Lewis when they found abandoned camps. The men noticed that around the base of some pine trees, the bark had been peeled off recently. Sacagawea told them that Indians used the bark to make many things, but they also used the soft wood underneath for sap and for food.[18]

The bark and the soft layer directly under it had long been used as a dietary supplement by Native Americans and even Laplanders in Scandinavia. The soft wood layers could be chewed and eaten much like meat jerky, or they could be dried and ground into flour for bread. The signs that Sacagawea saw likely indicated that the Indians who had been there recently either needed pitch for a canoe or were having difficulty finding enough food. It is possible, of course that they had merely been taking supplies, which they stored for lean times. Now that it was late spring, however, there was plenty of fish in the river to feed anyone living nearby.

Although the expedition sometimes ate fish, they only did so when necessary. During the entire journey, the men relied on red meat and viewed fish as a poor substitute. Sergeant John Ordway wrote in his journal that the river had "a considerable quantity of fish." He mused about what kinds they were but then added, "as we have a great plenty of meat we do not trouble ourselves for to catch fish."[19] This disregard for fish must have seemed very strange to Sacagawea. Her people relied heavily on fish for sustenance, and dried fish was an important staple of the long winter months.

One of the most troublesome factors the Corps of Discovery encountered on this first part of the journey was mosquitoes. Almost every day, several or all of the journal writers complained about the mosquitoes and gnats that tortured them daily. It must have been a challenge as a young mother to keep such insects away from her young baby. Many Native Americans used mud smeared on exposed skin for protection from insect bites. Perhaps Sacagawea used this remedy to keep little Jean-Baptiste healthy and free of insect bites. Sometimes, native people in the region also crushed the bulbs of wild onions to make a poultice for insect bites. The members of the corps survived the nights by sleeping under what they called "biers," or small frames covered with gauze.[20]

By far, however, the worst enemy was bad weather. The rain came often enough to cause dangerous floods and mud slides, and to keep the threat of ill health looming. For several days in this early part of the trip, it hailed so hard that they were forced to take shelter and wait out the storm as best they could. By the end of June and the very difficult and time-consuming portage around the falls, Lewis began to worry about how long the trip was taking:

> I begin to be extremely impatient to be off as the season is now wasting a pace. Nearly three months have now elapsed since we left Fort Mandan and not yet reached the Rocky Mountains. I am therefore fully persuaded that we shall not reach Fort Mandan again this season if we even return from the ocean to the Snake Indians (Shoshone).[21]

Lewis continued to worry about the pace of travel as the early summer progressed and turned into fall. His prediction was right; they would not return to Fort Mandan that same year and did not even begin the return journey from the ocean until the following spring.

In the midst of worry and difficulty, Lewis and Clark still managed to take copious notes about their surroundings, recording the strange sights and sounds they heard. In a few journal entries, Lewis mentioned a strange sound coming out of the mountains in the distance that sounded like artillery or gunshots. Since the weather was clear, it could not have been lightning. Lewis mused about the stories he had heard from the Minitares and other native peoples who said that the mountains spoke to each other in this way. Lewis did not want to believe what he called "superstitions" and instead comforted himself with information he gleaned from some of his men. They told him the sounds came from silver mines in the mountains that sometimes burst and cracked under certain weather conditions.[22] It must have been very strange to hear such mysterious noises and wonder about the American Indian stories. Sacagawea probably had her own traditions about these mountain noises. They were likely accompanied by stories of the mountains and their voices, stories that she murmured to her young son as she carried him on her back.

Through the threats of waterfalls and rapids, insect bites and strange illnesses, Sacagawea continued making her quiet contributions to the expedition on a daily basis. While raising her young son and protecting him from harm, she helped feed the expedition with her contributions of wild fruits and vegetables that she constantly gathered. Her roots and berries probably prevented more illness by bringing variety to a diet of mostly red meat. It took a large quantity of food to feed the Corps of Discovery. Lewis recorded that it took "four deer, an Elk and a deer, or one buffalo" to supply the group with food for 24 hours.[23] Sacagawea's contributions to their diet must have been very welcome, indeed. Soon, she would also provide the very important interpreting that Lewis and Clark needed in order to make the land journey from the Missouri River to the Columbia River.

## NOTES

1. Meriwether Lewis, May 14, 1805, in *The Journals of the Lewis and Clark Expedition*, ed. Gary E. Moulton (Lincoln: University of Nebraska Press, 1983–2001). Also made available online by University of Nebraska Press at http://lewisandclarkjournals.unl.edu/index.html. Listed hereafter as *JLC*.

2. Harold P. Howard, *Sacagawea* (Norman: University of Oklahoma Press, 1971), 32–33.

3. Lewis, May 10, 1805, *JLC*.

4. Lewis, May 11, 1805, *JLC*.

5. Ibid.

6. Lewis, May 12, 1805, *JLC*.

7. Lewis, May 14, 1805, *JLC*.

8. Roy Porter, *The Greatest Benefit to Mankind: A Medical History of Humanity from Antiquity to the Present* (New York: Harper Collins, 1997).

9. William Clark, June 11, 1805, *JLC*.

10. Howard, *Sacagawea*, 37.

11. Joseph Whitehouse, June 12, 1805, *JLC*.

12. Clark, June 16, 1805, *JLC*.

13. Whitehouse, June 16, 1805, *JLC*.

14. Lewis, June 18, 1805, *JLC*.

15. Clark, June 29, 1805, *JLC*.

16. Lewis, July 5, 1805, *JLC*.

17. Lewis, June 3, 1805, *JLC*.

18. Lewis, July 19, 1805, *JLC*.

19. John Ordway, June 5, 1805, *JLC*.

20. Howard, *Sacagawea*, 44–45.

21. Lewis, June 30, 1805, *JLC*.

22. Lewis, July 11, 1805, *JLC*.

23. Lewis, July 13, 1805, *JLC*.

# Chapter 5

# FAMILY REUNION

From the very beginning of her journey, Sacagawea knew she would finally see her people again after four or more years. She probably thought about what the meeting would be like, whom she would find well and who might not be. We do not know if she was afraid of the meeting or if she was really looking forward to it. She might have even wondered if her husband would offer to sell her back to her family, or if her family would even want to make such a transaction. There must have been many different thoughts swirling in her mind as time passed on the river.

## RECOGNIZING THE COUNTRY

By the end of July, almost a month after the Corps of Discovery managed to complete the difficult portage around the falls, Sacagawea began recognizing the landscape. This part of the country, in present-day Montana, was territory the Shoshones had traveled through on hunting trips. She told them that up the river at three forks, they would find her people.[1] How excited she must have been to recognize the area. They passed a small creek that flowed into the Missouri, and here, Sacagawea pointed out a bank where her people often came to gather some of the white-colored soil to use for paint. Lewis and Clark were both very happy to hear this good news from Sacagawea, but it would be more than three weeks before they finally found the Shoshones.

Meanwhile, Clark was feeling ill, and the entire corps felt exhausted. Since the river was now shallow, it was hard to row or use a sail. About half the party walked along the riverbanks each day, sometimes using towropes to pull the canoes. The other half used long poles to move the boats forward. Everyone was looking forward to a bit of overland travel on horseback. The plan was to purchase horses from the Shoshones and ride northwest to the Columbia River where they could resume their trip to the Pacific Ocean. Steep mountains blocked the path between the Missouri and the Columbia. It would not be possible to haul all their equipment and supplies through this portage without horses.

As they journeyed, Sacagawea might have told stories about her people, pointed out other landmarks along the way, and reassured Clark that her people would trade them horses. The journal writers do not reveal much about what these conversations might have been like. We are only left to imagine them. Perhaps someone asked about the white soil used for paint, and Sacagawea might have talked about other sources for paint that she had learned to gather as a child. She might have also talked about how many people from surrounding areas traded for Shoshone clothing. Sacagawea's people became known for their careful beadwork, and the various plant and soil dyes they made probably contributed to the reputation of their clothing.

At one point, Lewis wrote in his journal how much he feared they would again encounter dangerous falls. Only a few days earlier, Clark had to rescue Sacagawea's husband from being swept away in a rapid current of water. Others were feeling ill for one reason or another, and all were tired. However, Sacagawea reassured them that the river continued smoothly to where her people lived, and all Lewis could do was hope that she was right. As they passed into another chain of high mountains, Sacagawea told the group that they had reached another line of the Rockies.[2] The river filled with more rapids, and the riverbank itself became so rocky that many of the men towing the canoes cut their feet.

Before long, Sacagawea recognized the place where she had been captured as a child and carried off by the Hidatsas. She pointed out where she had hidden in the woods when they attacked her people and where she was finally snatched as she tried to run away with two other American Indian girls.[3] Although such an event was not particularly uncommon, Sacagawea must have felt very afraid when these strangers grabbed her and took her very faraway from her people and the land that she knew. She must have remembered these feelings as she passed the very site of her capture and began a journey home she had planned to take with her family when she was only 12.

Soon, the Corps of Discovery reached three forks, as Sacagawea had predicted. Now they had to decide which fork of the river to take in order to reach her people. Apparently, Sacagawea could not help them make this decision. After all, the Shoshone people often moved their camps in search of better hunting and fishing or for any number of reasons, including raids from Hidatsas and others. Once Lewis and Clark agreed to proceed up one of the river branches that they named after Thomas Jefferson, Sacagawea recognized more landmarks, confirming they had made the right choice. She saw a high plain that she remembered being near the summer camp of her people. She told them that the Shoshones called the hill "the beaver's head," and Lewis agreed that it did look a bit like the head of a beaver:

> She assures us that we shall either find her people on this river or on the river immediately west of its source; which from it's present sized cannot be very distant. As it is now all important with us to meet with those people as soon as possible, I determined to leave the charge of the party . . . to Capt. Clark; and proceed tomorrow with a small party . . . until I found the Indians . . . In short, it is my resolution to find them or some others, who have horses if it should cause me a trip of one month, for without horses we shall be obliged to leave a great part of our stores, of which, it appears to me that we have a stock already sufficiently small for the length of the voyage before us.[4]

From the above excerpt, it is obvious how vital the entire corps felt Sacagawea's presence to be and how weary and concerned Lewis was.

## MEETING CAMEAHWAIT

Finally, on August 11, Lewis encountered an Indian on a horse as he was exploring one of the river branches with several other men. The man seemed wary, but Lewis made efforts to give him a greeting. He called out "ta-ba-bone," which meant "white man," holding up some trade goods. However, the man rode away quickly, and Lewis felt frustrated and worried. Would this mean they had encountered hostile Indians and not Sacagawea's people? Would her people end up being unfriendly? Lewis made camp that night very worried about what the event signified.[5]

Two days later, they met up with more Indians—some women and children, who ran when Lewis and his men got close. He followed them down the trail and soon encountered a larger group of women with whom he managed to communicate after a few worried minutes. Lewis again told them that he was a white man, rolling up his shirtsleeve to show them his white skin. His skin had become sunburned during the journey, and he might have looked like an enemy from the surrounding area. He held up trade goods and finally was able to give these to the women and let them know he wanted to meet their chief. The women took Lewis and his men down the trail until they encountered a group of about sixty warriors on horseback. Lewis also showed them he was a white man, and the warriors then began greeting Lewis as a long-lost friend. He wrote in his journal that they had been expecting an attack from some Minitare Indians.[6]

Lewis soon discovered that the name of the chief was Cameahwait, who promptly set up an elaborate pipe ceremony to welcome the strangers into the camp. The native people shared what little food they had with Lewis and his men, but all they had were cakes made of dried berries. Lewis recorded that they tasted good, but he realized that he needed to help the Indians procure meat. About 20 or more of their people had been killed in a recent Minitare attack, which might have been part of the reason that they were short of food. The Corps of Discovery had had no luck hunting over the past few days and were not at all sure they could help the Indians. Lewis knew he had to help feed Cameahwait's people before he tried to trade for horses. The following day, Lewis observed the complicated way the Indians hunted the only plentiful game in the area—antelope. Since antelope run very fast, a single hunter on a horse cannot possibly keep up with one and shoot it with a bow and arrow. A large group of men on horseback, possibly as many as 20 or more hunters, would try to encircle a herd of antelope and isolate one or two that way. All of the warriors returned from the hunt exhausted that day and without a single antelope.

The next day, Lewis headed back with some of the Indians to meet up with Clark and the rest of the corps. He needed Sacagawea's presence as quickly as possible, since it was difficult communicating only in sign language. Meanwhile, Clark and the rest of the party continued up one of the branches, hoping to meet Lewis. Clark and Sacagawea both narrowly escaped being bitten by rattlesnakes sunning themselves on the riverbank. Clark's hunters were able to supply their group with meat, and finally, one of Lewis's men managed to kill a deer. Lewis was astounded when the entire group of American Indians immediately grabbed the dead deer, ripped it apart, and ate it raw on the spot. The next two deer the men found were devoured in the same way.[7]

Just before the two groups rejoined, Clark wrote in his journal that Charbonneau struck Sacagawea, for which Clark severely reprimanded him.[8] Nothing more is said about this incident, so there is no way of knowing why Charbonneau had become angry at his wife, whether he struck her often, or what Sacagawea might have felt or done after the fact. Was Charbonneau a violent man, or was he simply acting as any man would toward a wife who was viewed as his property? Did Sacagawea feel she deserved his violence, or was she angry? It is really impossible to answer these questions. Today, we see this incident in a much different light than people living in the early nineteenth century might have. However, Clark was angry at Charbonneau's action, so apparently he believed it was unwarranted. Lewis later recorded the same incident in his journal after Clark told him about it. Both men found it important enough to mention.

Within the next day or two, Sacagawea appears in the journals again, providing "a great number of fine berries" to supplement the fresh game.[9] What must it have been like to be this American Indian woman, risking her health on a rough journey, raising a young baby on the trail, anticipating a meeting with her lost family, while surviving rattlesnakes and being struck by her husband? Yet, she continued doing what she had always done for the Corps of Discovery and gathered wild food.

Finally, on August 17, Lewis and Clark met up with each other, and Sacagawea saw her people again. The most surprising thing was that Cameahwait was Sacagawea's brother. Lewis was astounded by this good fortune. When Sacagawea recognized her brother, she must have been overcome with emotion. Lewis wrote that it was a very moving experience to watch the reunion, especially when Sacagawea saw the Indian woman who had been captured with her as a girl. This woman had escaped and found her way back to her people, unlike Sacagawea. Later that same afternoon, Sacagawea began serving the main task for which she had been brought on the trip—interpreting. She helped inform her people that Lewis and Clark wanted to trade for horses and that befriending these white men would create a good trading relationship for the Shoshones in the future.[10]

As Sacagawea interpreted for them, Lewis and Clark told the Shoshones that they needed horses to complete their journey. They also asked them for information about the land and the Columbia River to the north. Lewis felt he received reasonable information and that these people were being open and honest with him. The Shoshones really wanted guns and ammunition. They naturally felt that this would help them when hunting the swift antelope and would also help them defend themselves against their enemies in the east, who already had such weapons. When Lewis informed them that he could not trade weapons at this point, Cameahwait was disappointed but accepted the promise that the white people would return and bring guns.[11]

As Lewis talked and bartered for horses, he observed the Shoshone people. He seemed very astonished that although they lived in poverty, they were generally cheerful people and generous to each other and to strangers. He also observed that the people lived in what he considered an equal society, where even the chiefs were merely men of influence, not of absolute power. He did observe, however, that men were very much in control of their wives and children, and that some men had several wives. Some fathers bartered or "sold" their daughters, sometimes to much older men. In fact, Lewis observed, Sacagawea had been promised to a man more than twice her age before she was captured.

Lewis also recorded that Sacagawea's husband stepped forward and claimed her as his wife, although he already had two other wives. Then he "said that as she had had a child by another man, who was Charbono [sic], that he did not want her."[12] Lewis might have been relieved by this decision, but he did not think the Shoshones treated their women very well. He criticized how the men seemed to do very little work except to hunt and fish, while the women cooked, built shelter, cared for children, gathered food, and did so many other daily tasks. Even though Lewis did not think very much of Charbonneau, he might have thought Sacagawea had a better life with the French trader than she would have had with her people.

## HELP FROM FRIENDS

Every day or two, Lewis managed to barter for a couple of horses, as he continued communicating with Cameahwait and his people. They traveled on, met other groups of Shoshones, and bartered for more horses as they went along. Lewis recorded at one such meeting that the Shoshones there had no food, and he made them a meal of beans and corn, which they really enjoyed. Cameahwait said that he had never tasted anything better, except for the lump of sugar that his sister had given him. Apparently, Sacagawea had saved a small lump of sugar from their stores. He was amazed by it, and all the Shoshones wished they had food like the white men carried. Lewis told the Shoshones that in the future, a good trading relationship with the white people would mean they could move to land better for growing such foods themselves. This sounded very encouraging to the Indians.[13]

As the expedition moved north to the Shoshone camp there, Lewis calculated what he would need for the rest of the journey. Besides other stores, he estimated he would need 25 horses in all. So far, he had managed to purchase 9 horses and a mule, of which he was very proud. In the meantime, Lewis recorded his observations about the flint tools the Shoshones used for almost all purposes and described the way they made weapons and shields for battle. Clark explored two nearby streams for possible water passages through the mountains to the Columbia and recorded

the terrain and his estimations of finding trees suitable for making canoes. All the while, Sacagawea accompanied her husband on the trail and
served as an interpreter for Lewis as he quizzed the Shoshones for information and bartered for horses.

On August 25, however, Lewis felt he had narrowly avoided disaster for
the expedition. He found out that afternoon that a runner had been sent to
tell the Shoshones at the northern camp to head south and meet with the
Shoshones there. The hunters planned to travel south to buffalo country,
leaving Lewis and Clark's expedition stranded with too few horses and no
help traversing the mountains. When Charbonneau finally told Lewis this
news, it was hours after he had first learned about it from Sacagawea. She
must have assumed that her husband would tell Lewis in a timely fashion
and probably continued visiting with others in the tribe or caring for her
young son. When Lewis heard that Charbonneau had waited hours to give
him this critical news, he was very angry and could barely talk to Charbonneau without shouting. Then he called the Shoshone chiefs together,
smoked a pipe, and angrily accused them of going back on their word.

Lewis carefully explained why it was important for the expedition to be
able to trade for horses and to have all the help they could find to cross
the mountains. He also explained all the advantages the Shoshones would
have from a good relationship with the white man. The chiefs agreed and
said Cameahwait had sent the runner. Cameahwait admitted it was true
and apologized for his actions but explained that he was tired of seeing
his people hungry and had ordered the hunting party. He recalled the
message, and Lewis breathed a sigh of relief. Once again, Charbonneau
confirmed Lewis's opinion that the Frenchman was not terribly useful to
the expedition and sometimes quite a liability.[14]

In spite of this scare, the party soon reached the northern camp and
managed to trade for more horses until they had 29 and a mule. Then
they bid good-bye to Sacagawea's people and headed north toward the
Columbia with their new horses and an Indian guide named Toby. Then a
very difficult part of the journey began. While they had experienced many
challenges already, such as sickness, mosquitoes, rapids and falls, spilled
boats, and lack of meat, the mountains would prove the toughest phase.
They were unforgiving, and the journey very slow. Sacagawea must have
also experienced the emotional pain of leaving her family and people behind once again, this time by choice. There is no mention in the journals
of her debating about staying, or asking to do so. Apparently, her loyalties
were bound to her husband and his employment by the expedition.

Yet, the mountain journey must have been made all the more difficult
by this farewell. Sacagawea could not know whether she would ever see

her people again. Perhaps Clark, who seemed to talk with her the most, promised she would see them again on the return trip. If anyone made such promises, they were not recorded in the journals. It was also true that Sacagawea's life was now very different than it would have been had she never been captured. The husband to whom she had been promised did not want her now, and perhaps she felt she would always be treated as an outsider among her own people. Love for her husband might also have kept her in the expedition, and concern about her son may also have been a factor. Charbonneau might have forced Sacagawea to leave her child with him if she chose to stay with the Shoshones. It was very common in western societies in the early nineteenth century to grant custody to the father, if he wanted it.

While the journals do not mention Sacagawea for a few months, one can imagine her struggles along with the rest of the Corps of Discovery as they made the very difficult traverse across the Bitterroot Range of mountains in present-day Montana. The summer was ending, and snow would soon be on the way. Meanwhile, they struggled with cold rain, very rocky and steep paths, and worn-out horses. One became crippled, and another two were simply too lean and worn out to carry baggage. It soon became clear that they did not have nearly enough horses for the journey.

Thankfully, they encountered more American Indians in early September—the Flatheads. They were friendly, shared their store of berries and roots, and sold Lewis 11 much-needed horses. This encounter cheered the low spirits of the expedition as they journeyed north. Finally, they turned west and once again began to cross over the high Bitterroot Mountains into present-day Idaho. Toby, the Indian guide, lost his way and took them three miles off course before he realized his mistake. Some more horses became lame or ill, and the expedition began to run very low on food. Just to make matters nearly unbearable for Clark, a horse stumbled and rolled on top of his writing desk, smashing it.[15]

It was one day after another of cold, snow, rain, sometimes-unexpected heat, and always a rough trail and stumbling horses. Sacagawea must have found it very challenging caring for a young child on such a journey. Little Jean-Baptiste must have spent most of his time riding in the cradle board on his mother's back as she struggled up the path on foot. Her main purpose on the expedition was over, but she had little choice now but to journey on with them. She did want to see the Pacific Ocean she heard them talking about, but may have doubted whether it was worth the trip. Most of the other men with Lewis and Clark also wondered if the entire journey had been worth the trouble.

As they started experiencing real hunger in the absence of good hunting, they again encountered American Indians—the Nez Perce. The main leader, named Twisted Hair, welcomed the expedition and shared food with them. Lewis and Clark spoke at length with Twisted Hair and passed out peace medals and other gifts. Twisted Hair drew some maps of the rivers ahead for the men and showed them the location of falls and rapids. However, as the men ate more berries, roots, and fish than they were used to eating, they probably ate too much and too quickly. Several became ill, keeping Clark quite busy handing out medicines.[16]

Finally, they reached the edge of the Clearwater River that would run into the larger Columbia. As some of the men rested from illness, others who were strong enough made canoes for the rest of the trip. From this point, the plan was to travel downstream to the ocean without the need for poles, towlines, and sails. The Nez Perce promised to watch the horses and keep them for the return trip. Others hunted and gathered meat for the journey, and by early October, the expedition was once again traveling by water. The long portage had been difficult and much harder than the group had anticipated. If it had not been for the translation help of Sacagawea, the corps would never have made it through the mountains.

Although they had Indian maps and some information about the rest of their journey to the ocean, things did not go as smoothly as they had hoped. As they traveled down the Clearwater to the Snake River, they found far more rapids than expected. The canoes often became stuck on rocks, and the cargo was sometimes dumped into the water. One day, they capsized a boat of supplies and had to spend time finding canisters of gunpowder lost on the river bottom and drying them out by a fire on the bank. However, the good part of this journey was the supply of fish. They began to encounter Indians fishing along the banks of the river. Once they finally entered the Columbia River, they met a man named Chief Yellepet, who was probably a Cayuse, as well as some others known as Sokulks.

On October 19, not long after meeting Chief Yellepet, Clark inadvertently frightened some Indians living along the river when he fired his gun at a bird overhead. It took him a while to explain through hand signals that he meant them no harm, and that his gun was not some kind of supernatural magic that would hurt them. Nothing seemed to persuade them otherwise until Lewis finally caught up with Clark and brought Sacagawea and her baby into the village. When they saw her with her child, the Indians immediately calmed down. They must have decided that the group was harmless if a woman and child traveled with them. Lewis mentioned in his journal how very advantageous it was to have Sacagawea and little Jean-Baptiste along at such times.[17]

After eating and smoking with the Indians, two of the men of the expedition played a violin they had brought. The Indians enjoyed the music very much and stayed at their campfires all night, visiting. Now that they were again on water, they could cover many more miles in a single day. On October 19, Clark noted that they had traveled 36 miles.[18] However, they also ran so short of game that they often bartered for dogs from the Indians they continued to meet along the way. Some of these Indians knew a few words of English from previous encounters with white men along the coast. They also knew how to bargain for higher prices than other Indians further inland. The group encountered more rapids and some difficult portages. They were now in present-day Oregon and knew the ocean was close.

Finally, on November 7, the expedition heard and eventually sighted the Pacific Ocean.[19] Sacagawea must have been filled with wonder at such an amazing sight. The rest of the party was relieved that they had reached their goal but also worried that winter would settle in soon. The corps explored along the north and south banks of the Columbia in order to settle upon a good location for their winter camp. They knew they would need very good shelter for the snowy months and a place to collect and store food they would need.

## NOTES

1. Joseph Whitehouse, July 22, 1805, in *The Journals of the Lewis and Clark Expedition,* ed. Gary E. Moulton (Lincoln: University of Nebraska Press, 1983–2001). Also made available online by University of Nebraska Press at http://lewisandclarkjournals.unl.edu/index.html. Listed hereafter as *JLC.*

2. Patrick Gass, July 25, 1805, *JLC.*

3. John Ordway, July 30, 1805, *JLC.*

4. Meriwether Lewis, August 8, 1805, *JLC.*

5. Lewis, August 11, 1805, *JLC.*

6. Lewis, August 13, 1805, *JLC.*

7. Lewis, August 16, 1805, *JLC.*

8. William Clark, August 14, 1805, *JLC.*

9. Whitehouse, August 16, 1805, *JLC.*

10. Lewis, August 17, 1805, *JLC.*

11. Ibid.

12. Lewis, August 19, 1805, *JLC.*

13. Lewis, August 22, 1805, *JLC.*

14. Lewis, August 25, 1805, *JLC.*

15. Clark, September 15, 1805, *JLC.*

16. Clark, September 24, 1805, *JLC.*

17. Lewis, October 19, 1805, *JLC.*

18. Ibid.

19. Clark, November 7, 1805, *JLC.*

# Chapter 6

# THE DESTINATION

Half of the journey was now over, and it was time for the Corps of Discovery to rest for the winter. Sacagawea now had a young son who would soon be crawling, if he had the opportunity. The winter was bitter cold, however, and Sacagawea and her family would be sharing small, rough cabins with Lewis and Clark during the cold and dark winter months.

## THE PACIFIC OCEAN

When the expedition first sighted the ocean, the journal writers talked about the joy people felt at finally reaching their goal. They had traveled about 4,100 miles since they left St. Louis and had every right to feel relieved and happy.[1] They were also now finding much more wild game, specifically geese and other fowl and were eating much better. Conditions, however, were far from excellent. As they traveled up and down the banks of the Columbia looking for a good place to build a winter camp, many of the expedition members became motion sick from the waves, and they were all miserable from the weather. As is normal for that region, especially in November, it was cold and rainy almost every day, and the fog often made it hard for them to see where they were going. All the journal entries from this period sound almost as dismal as the entries from the difficult mountain portage. They were constantly short on drinkable water because the river water so near the ocean was really too salty to drink.

As the group tried first one camping location and then another, they almost invariably woke in the morning with wet bedding and canoes that were in danger of being swept away. On November 13, Lewis made a

cryptic note in his journal that the "Squar is displeased with me. . . ."
What she was upset about was not clear from the journal. He went on
to mention a root called *wap-too*, which tasted like a potato.[2] Perhaps
Sacagawea was simply unhappy with the dangerous camp location or that
Lewis had not brought any of the roots he mentioned back to camp. Sacagawea wanted to make sure that the expedition had plenty of good
food, and she was constantly supplementing their diet with some kind of
fresh root or berry, even in this unfamiliar country.

During the rainy and cold weeks of November, the expedition traded
with neighboring American Indians who asked very high prices for goods,
much to Lewis and Clark's dismay. Many American Indian females came
by the camps, offering to sell themselves for the night. Some guns and
other items disappeared, apparently stolen from the men by the Indian
women who came around. Clark threatened some of the Indians who
came to trade, saying that if anything else went missing, or if he caught
anyone stealing, he would not hesitate to shoot him or her.[3] This kind
of attitude was very uncharacteristic for Clark; he must have truly felt
harassed and angry at the expedition's losses and the potential for more.
Guns, of course, were critical for their survival, not just for protection.
Without guns and ammunition, the expedition might starve or become
completely dependent upon their Indian neighbors.

One day, a chief of the people who lived at the mouth of the Columbia
met with Lewis and offered him friendship. He learned that these American
Indians were called the Chinook. Lewis hoped he would be able to establish a good trading relationship with them to help the expedition manage the long winter ahead. Both Lewis and Clark, however, complained in
their journals that any time a Chinook gave them a gift, they expected far
more than the gift was worth in return. One Chinook came to trade and
wore a beautiful coat of otter fur, which both Lewis and Clark thought was
the most beautiful fur they had ever seen. Desperate to trade for this coat,
Lewis offered the man many things, but the man refused to give up his coat.
Finally, they offered him a blue-beaded belt that belonged to Sacagawea.
Blue beads were very much in demand by the Chinook. They considered
them symbols of a chief. The blue-beaded belt finally sealed the trade.[4]

There is no mention in the journals about how Sacagawea felt about
the trade. She wore the belt around her waist all the way from her home
among the Mandans to the Pacific Ocean. She had never offered to trade
it before, and she may not have wanted to then, but the journals make
no mention of this issue. Sacagawea might have offered it willingly, seeing how much Lewis and Clark wanted the coat. While there is little
evidence that she had warm feelings for Lewis, she was close to Clark

and grateful to him for the attention he showed her son. She might have offered the belt as a way to thank Clark for his kindness. It is also possible that the two leaders of the expedition begged her to trade the belt. Lewis recorded in his journal the following day that he gave Sacagawea a blue coat in exchange for the beaded belt.[5]

Now that trading had proven quite expensive, Lewis and Clark began seriously planning for their winter stay. Clark noted in his journal that he doubted the Indians had enough food to supply the expedition, even if they had been willing to trade. So he began planning elk hunts and salt making out of the ocean water.[6] This salt could be used both as seasoning and for preserving meat. That same day, Lewis recorded an interesting event—a vote. Most of the time, Lewis and Clark ran their expedition like the military, with all decisions handed down from them to their men. This time, however, Lewis recorded a vote of the group on where to make the winter camp. Lewis recorded that most voted to cross to the south side of the river and find a place to camp there instead of where they were on the north side. Everyone voted, including the slave York, and Lewis recorded that even Sacagawea had her vote. She voted for a place that had "plenty of potatoes" or the edible root wap-too.[7]

This vote was a unique and special moment in American history. It was the first recorded vote in the United States by a woman and by a black slave. This was truly an American moment, even though it would be a very long time before either women or African Americans would be able to vote. York had been raised with Clark and been his slave since childhood. Clark respected York, but did treat him as any master would. In spite of how close they were, York continued to be treated as a slave and would not receive his freedom until more than a decade after the expedition was over. Yet, at this time, he did at least have a vote.

When Lewis recorded Sacagawea's vote, he called her Janey. Apparently, this had become her nickname, although it does not appear elsewhere in the journals. Clark used the nickname again in a letter he wrote to Charbonneau after the expedition. Such a nickname certainly demonstrated how fondly Lewis and Clark regarded Sacagawea. Whether they asked for Sacagawea's vote or whether she offered it on her own, it was an important enough opinion for Lewis to duly record with the others. He made no further comment on her choice but probably found it a sound one, perhaps even a predictable opinion from the woman he now called Janey.

The wet and soggy days dragged on, and the expedition finally met some Clatsop Indians, after whom they would name their winter quarters. All their clothes and blankets were rotting and falling apart because they were always wet, and trading for new ones from the Indians proved too

expensive. Although they were out of most of the food stores they had
brought with them, Sacagawea had set aside a small amount of flour to
bake bread for her little son Jean-Baptiste. Even this little store had gotten wet, so Sacagawea made it into bread and gave some to Clark, who
always seemed to be watching out for her.[8]

## WINTERING AT FORT CLATSOP

As Lewis explored down the river for a campsite, Sacagawea showed
Clark and the others how to boil elk bones into grease or tallow after all
the meat and marrow had been used.[9] The men must have been impressed
with her ingenuity and ability to make useful things out of seemingly
nothing. This was, after all, how her people had survived over the years
without access to manufactured goods, just as Europeans had in earlier
times. Finally, Lewis returned and told the group he had found a good
place for a winter camp. Several days later, the party traveled to this inlet
where there seemed to be many elk. The men began cutting logs to make
cabins, while Clark took some men to the seashore to make salt for preserving meat. They ended up with eight small log cabins, about 16 by 30
feet, which they surrounded with a stockade. They named their winter
camp Fort Clatsop, after the local Indians.

In one of the cabins, a very large tree stump was too hard to remove.
Clark used this stump for his writing desk.[10] After they had raised the logs
to the proper height, they had to construct watertight roofs and chink the
walls. Each day, the journal writers record work being done on the cabins through most of December. In addition, while they were working to
finishing the cabins, the rain continued to keep them all wet, miserable,
and often sick with colds. Clark recorded that the leather lodge that he,
Lewis, Sacagawea, Toussaint, and Jean-Baptiste all shared during most of
the journey was now rotting and full of holes, incapable of keeping out
the incessant rain.[11] Hunting parties were particularly wet and miserable,
but everyone kept working hard. The group built one cabin to be a storage
house for meat they hoped to find and preserve. It was impossible to keep
extra meat from spoiling in all the rain.

Finally, on Christmas Day, the Corps of Discovery moved into their
finished cabins and began drying out their supplies. It had taken almost
three miserably wet weeks to finish the cabins and everyone was more
than ready for the shelter. The men were building and working in the rain
and even some snow before the fort was completed. Sacagawea must have
found it difficult to keep her young son dry and healthy in such weather
with so little shelter. She must have felt as joyful as the others must when

they all celebrated Christmas by moving into dry rooms with rough bunks hewn from trees. Lewis and Clark gave each of the men who were smokers some tobacco as a Christmas gift and handkerchiefs to those who were not. Clark recorded receiving some nice presents from Lewis and the other officers, and a gift of two dozen white weasel tails from Sacagawea.[12] Perhaps Clark made a small cloak or scarf with these warm tails.

Christmas dinner was elk that apparently was not very good. Each journal writer recorded the lackluster dinner but still spoke of gratitude for finally having warm places to sleep. However, they apparently had trouble with fleas. Clark wrote about having trouble and hardly sleeping at night because of them. They must have come from their horses or the wild game they hunted. As the last few days of December dragged by, the men finished building chimneys for their huts and gates for the fort entrance. They informed the Indians who came to trade every day that they would shut the gates every evening at sunset and ask all of the Indians to leave at that time. Apparently, the Indians did not like this idea very much but cooperated.[13]

On January 1, Lewis and Clark enjoyed a firearms salute from their men and ate a meal of elk meat and "wap-too" roots, a meal that was better than what they had eaten on Christmas Day. Later that day, Lewis and Clark decided to set up specific rules for how the fort would run while they were there. Everyone except the cook and interpreters would serve on guard duty and hunting expeditions. There would always be a sergeant and three privates on guard duty at all times, and everyone was to treat the Indians with respect. No one, however, was to trade any metal items to the Indians without specific permission. The men must have been worried about their tools and supplies, so the specific list of forbidden items included all metal tools such as knives and axes, all firearms, and ammunition.[14]

Life soon settled into a rather boring routine of hunting, guard duty, occasional trading, and other tasks such as mending and making salt. On January 6, 1806, Lewis recorded the only complaint heard from Sacagawea during the entire journey. While some of the men were at the seashore making salt, some Indians told them of a very large, beached whale farther up the coast. When Lewis heard the news, he decided to take some men with him to see the whale and bring back some of its blubber. Sacagawea must have asked to go and was probably told she should stay at the fort, safe and warm. She must have protested, because Lewis recorded the following:

> The Indian woman was very importunate to be permitted to go, and was therefore indulged; she observed that she had traveled a long way with us to see the great waters, and that now

that monstrous fish was also to be seen, she thought it very
hard she could not be permitted to see either.[15]

Thus, Sacagawea was taken along on the trip and saw the ocean. When
they found the beached whale, all that was left was a giant skeleton, and
they were all disappointed. No one recorded Sacagawea's reaction to seeing this skeleton or the ocean, but she must have been amazed at such
sights. Upon arriving at the ocean, Clark wrote, "from this point I beheld
the grandest and most pleasing prospects which my eyes ever surveyed, in
my frount [sic] a boundless Ocean; to the N. and N. E. the coast as far as
my sight Could be extended."[16] It was an awesome sight to everyone who
saw it.

After the initial excitement of seeing the ocean and finishing Fort
Clapsot, life settled into a semicomfortable routine for the Corps of Discovery. Their cabins were warm and dry, but game was scarce that winter.
The journal writers often mention worries about low meat supplies and
some days of fasting. Lewis and Clark spent their spare time writing up
reports about local American Indian culture and the flora and fauna. The
men took their turns with guard duty, hunting, and salt making, and in
their spare time, they dressed deerskins for clothes. They needed to make
many moccasins and other clothing for their return trip, as well as preserve and dry as much meat as possible for lean times.

Although there was much work to be done, there were constant visits
at the fort by local Indians who wanted to trade. Gradually, the expedition began to run out of trade goods until by March, they had only a
handful left and were worried about how to obtain necessary trade goods
from the Indians. However, one so-called trade good was always available to the men—the local Indian women who willingly offered to sleep
with them. Although both Lewis and Clark discouraged these encounters,
they inevitably occurred, as well as sickness from venereal disease. Lewis
treated his men for such diseases with mercury, which he was grateful
he had brought. He marveled that the native people, although carrying
syphilis and gonorrhea, lived much longer and healthier lives than whites
who had contracted venereal diseases.[17]

On February 1, both Lewis and Clark mentioned the marking of one
month of winter in the fort, and the gladness that spring was thus one
month closer. Boredom must have been a problem, but both Lewis and
Clark made many observations of the local Indians and recorded their
clothing and other habits in detail. One day, both men wrote at length
about the love the Indians had of gambling or games of risk. One game that
Lewis described consisted of placing some object in the hand, showing it

to all, then switching hands back and forth very fast while singing a special song made just for this game. When the person was tired of singing
and switching hands, the other player picked which hand the object was
in. If they guessed right, they won the object.[18]

Although all the journal writers usually recorded the actions of the
American Indians without a lot of judgment, negative attitudes appear in
the records while the expedition was at Fort Clapsot. The reason for this
change was likely the fact that the Indians along the coast were much
more accustomed to whites and took opportunities to steal when they
could. They also charged much more for their trade goods than the Plains
Indians had. Lewis reveals in one journal entry his ongoing suspicions of
the Indians and the need never to trust them completely:

> We never suffer parties of such number to remain within the
> fort all night; for notwithstanding their apparent friendly dis-
> position, their great avarice and hope of plunder might induce
> them to be treacherous. At all events, we determined always
> to be on our guard as much as the nature of our situation will
> permit us, and never place ourselves at the mercy of any sav-
> ages. We well know, that the treachery of the aborigines of
> America and the too great confidence of our country men in
> their sincerity and friendship, has caused the destruction of
> many hundreds of us . . . the well known treachery of the na-
> tives by no means entitle them to such confidence . . . that our
> preservation depends on never losing sight of this trait in their
> character, and being always prepared to meet it in whatever
> shape it may present itself.[19]

One wonders how Lewis managed to place such trust in Sacagawea, or if
he ever stopped seeing her as a potentially dangerous savage.

Most of the time, Lewis and Clark managed hunting parties, oversaw
the drying of meat and collection of salt, traded with the Indians, and
plotted their return journey. Lewis, using Clark's carefully constructed
maps and information from the Indians, realized that the expedition
had lengthened the journey on the way out unnecessarily. To find the
headwaters of the Missouri, they had turned south, increasing the time
they would spend crossing the difficult mountains to the Columbia.
Now that they realized this fact, the return journey would be easier with
a shorter mountain portage.[20]

Within the very small fort, Sacagawea spent the winter gathering wild
roots and raising her young son. Jean-Baptiste was now probably six to

eight months old and was likely growing rapidly, beginning to crawl his way to any interesting object he could find. It must have been a challenge, knowing what to do with a young baby within such very small cabins in the winter. There were no other women for Sacagawea to talk to, except for those who came to visit the fort. Some of them spoke English, having learned from English or American traders who came to the coast by ship. Sacagawea must have marveled at their interesting stories of encounters with these men who sailed the vast ocean she had just seen for the first time.

In fact, all members of the expedition were interested in hearing about the ocean-going vessels. Lewis and Clark hoped that they would encounter such a vessel that could take maybe one or two of them back home via sea, along with reports and specimens. They likely missed one of these ships by mere weeks, and no others came all winter long. Lewis and Clark decided that they had to begin their return journey when spring came, rather than waiting any longer for alternative transportation.[21] They had already been gone nearly two years by the time they headed back home. President Thomas Jefferson, as well as almost everyone else, assumed that they were dead.

Meanwhile, the group began to gather what they needed in terms of dried meat and salt. The salt makers managed to produce two kegs by the end of February, when Lewis decided that they had enough. The weather continued to be rainy and snowy for months, and several men became ill near the end of February. Lewis decided it was probably influenza, not just the common cold. He was, however, gratified to see that they were all slowly improving. No one struggled with very bad illness during the cold winter, in spite of the sometimes short rations and always miserable weather.

One day in late February, some Clapsot Indians arrived at the fort with a large number of hats they had made for the expedition. Lewis described these hats as made out of cedar bark with grass ornamentation. He was very impressed with the hats and noted that they were very tightly woven and waterproof. He declared the Clapsots more inventive than most American Indians.[22] Once the elk became scarce, the group ate more and more fish, which was very plentiful and which the Indians often brought for trade. The men were not used to eating fish, but now they actually seemed to relish it. They added fishing parties to the hunting parties they sent out each day and were counting the days until April 1, when they planned to begin their eastward journey. By early March, they were out of tobacco; of the 33 members of the expedition, only 7 did not smoke. The men now tried to use crab-tree bark for smoking, instead of tobacco.[23]

They had all been busy making moccasins and clothing out of elk and deerskins. Sacagawea probably spent a lot of her time making these moccasins, capes, and shirts. Since the leather moccasins wore out in a very short period, the 31 members now had on hand 358 pairs of moccasins: at least 10 pairs for each person.[24] Lewis was determined that his men would not go barefoot as they had for some stretches of time on the journey west. Sacagawea had grown up making clothing and moccasins out of skins. She probably carefully taught the men how to measure, cut, and stitch them in the best possible way. Although we do not know how she interacted with these men while in the fort for so long, she might have told them her childhood stories while she worked. This would have been the way she learned to make moccasins—while listening to the stories of her mother, grandmother, aunts, and other women of the nation.

One of the things that Lewis hoped the men were not busy doing was having sexual relationships with the Indian women who regularly came to the fort for that purpose. One day, Lewis wrote of the return of a number of Chinook women who had visited sometime before:

> We were visited this afternoon by Delashshelwitt, a Chinnook Chief, his wife and six women of his nation which the old baud his wife had brought for market. This was the same party that had communicated the venereal to so many of my party in November last, and of which they have finally recovered. I therefore gave the men a particular charge with respect to them which they promised me to observe.[25]

The women often came to offer themselves to the men in exchange for trade goods. Apparently, they thought nothing of this behavior, much to Lewis and Clark's distress.

Another distressing condition to Lewis was the small amount of trade goods they now possessed. They needed to buy horses along the way, and they really did not have enough to purchase canoes for the first part of the trip. Lewis wrote in his journal that since the Clapsots charged too much for a canoe, the expedition would simply take one in payment for some six elks the Clapsots had stolen from the expedition hunters. This was not his usual behavior toward the American Indians. All members of the expedition had been carefully instructed to treat the Indians they met with respect, as they were ambassadors to them from the "new rulers" of the land. On this one occasion, however, Lewis seemed vexed enough not to give stealing a canoe a second thought. He felt the Clapsots owed the expedition a canoe, at the very least.

Toward the end of March, as the group began to prepare for their departure, Lewis and Clark wrote up lists of the members of the party and gave these lists to several different chiefs in the area, posting one in their fort. The list stated the date they had arrived and built the fort and the purpose of their journey, just in case they did not make it home. Someday, someone might discover the list and know the expedition had reached the Pacific. One of the chiefs might even give the list to an English trader in port one day. In this way, Lewis and Clark hoped to leave behind a record of their journey, along with a few maps.

Eager to be on their way, the group decided to leave the fort around March 20, but bad weather delayed their departure. There were also several men who were ill, and canoes needed to be strengthened. They repaired their guns, grateful they had brought some spare parts with them for that purpose. Some hunters were sent up ahead as they waited a few days for the weather to improve. Sacagawea must have had a lot to do also, getting herself and her young toddler ready for the journey. Jean-Baptiste was just over a year old and probably walking. Sacagawea must have had her hands full keeping him out of mischief while sewing clothing and moccasins for him, herself, and her husband and possibly helping other members of the expedition sew theirs as well. Clothing for the toddler would be perhaps bulkier and more difficult to carry than clothing for an infant. Now that Jean-Baptiste was older, he would also be heavier to carry.

On the first half of the journey, Sacagawea had carried her small child in a cradle board strapped to her back. It is not clear whether he was still small enough for her to carry him in this way. Perhaps his father and some of the other expedition members helped carry him from time to time when they were not riding in a canoe or on horseback. Now Sacagawea would have to watch him more carefully to make sure he did not reach out and topple into the water. She would have to make sure he did not put plants in his mouth that might make him sick. He might even have some fears beginning to develop. Sacagawea would now spend more energy reassuring her young son and keeping him calm and happy on the journey. Yet, she did not complain and seemed as ready as ever for the journey. She was probably eager to get Jean-Baptiste back home where he could live a more normal life for a toddler. Everyone was ready to be home as soon as possible.

# NOTES

1. Harold P. Howard, *Sacagawea* (Norman: University of Oklahoma Press, 1971), 83.

2. Meriwether Lewis, November 13, 1805, in *The Journals of the Lewis and Clark Expedition*, ed. Gary E. Moulton (Lincoln: University of Nebraska Press,

1983–2001). Also made available online by University of Nebraska Press at http://lewisandclarkjournals.unl.edu/index.html. Listed hereafter as *JLC*.

   3. William Clark, November 15, 1805, *JLC*.

   4. Clark, November 20, 1805, *JLC*.

   5. Lewis, November 21, 1805, *JLC*.

   6. Clark, November 24, 1805, *JLC*.

   7. Lewis, November 24, 1805, *JLC*.

   8. Clark, November 30, 1805, *JLC*.

   9. Clark, December 3, 1805, *JLC*.

   10. Howard, *Sacagawea*, 85–86.

   11. Clark, December 17, 1805, *JLC*.

   12. Clark, December 25, 1805, *JLC*.

   13. Clark, December 30, 1805, *JLC*.

   14. Lewis, January 1, 1806, *JLC*.

   15. Lewis, January 6, 1806, *JLC*.

   16. Clark, January 8, 1806, *JLC*.

   17. Lewis, January 27, 1806, *JLC*.

   18. Lewis, February 2, 1806, *JLC*.

   19. Lewis, February 20, 1806, *JLC*.

   20. Lewis, February 14, 1806, *JLC*.

   21. Howard, *Sacagawea*, 91–92.

   22. Lewis, February 22, 1806, *JLC*.

   23. Patrick Gass, March 7, 1806, *JLC*.

   24. Clark, March 12, 1806, *JLC*.

   25. Lewis, March 15, 1806, *JLC*.

*Sacagawea with Lewis and Clark. Nineteenth-century illustration by W. S. Chapman. Eon Images.*

*Sculpted by Leonard Crunelle in 1910, this statue stands in front of the state capital building in Bismark, North Dakota. A replica was made in 2003 for the National Statuary Hall in Washington, DC. Courtesy of Alamy Images.*

William Clark (left) and Meriwether Lewis (center) with Sacagawea, detail from Lewis and Clark at Three Forks, oil painting by Edgar Samuel Paxson, 1912. Many early depictions of Sacagawea erroneously portrayed her as a guide, arm lifted, pointing the way for Lewis and Clark. The Granger Collection, New York.

Stamp issued by the U.S. Postal Service in 1954 to commemorate the 150th anniversary of the Lewis and Clark Expedition. The Granger Collection, New York.

This statue stands in the Sacajawea Memorial in Salmon, Idaho, and was sculpted by Agnes Vincen Talbot in 2003. A duplicate stands in front of the Idaho Historical Museum in Boise. © John Elk III/ Alamy.

# Chapter 7

# RETURN TRIP

On March 23, 1806, the Corps of Discovery finally left their winter quarters at Fort Clapsot on the Columbia River near the Pacific Ocean. It had been a long four months in the very rainy and cold climate of present-day Oregon and Washington. During the winter, the men recorded only 15 days of sunshine. No wonder they were all eager to head out as early as possible. They were all homesick, for they had now been journeying for over a year. Sacagawea was probably also eager for another chance to see her people, the Shoshones, on the return journey. Did she contemplate staying with them?

## HEADING EAST

With plenty of new, dry clothing and good canoes, Lewis and Clark's expedition headed back up the Columbia River toward drier country as quickly as possible. On the second day out, one of the Indians claimed a canoe that Lewis had taken from the Clapsots. He was willing to trade it for an elk skin, however, so the expedition kept their canoe. Both Sergeants Ordway and Gass mentioned the quality of this canoe in their journals. They concluded that the Indians along the western part of the Columbia were the most skilled canoe makers in the world.[1]

This early part of the trip was upstream and difficult, since the heavy rains and the beginning of winter melts made the water levels in the river very high.[2] Good canoes were critical for navigating the rough waters. Small canoes were even better, Lewis and Clark decided. So they decided to trade out their larger canoes for smaller ones along the way upriver, and they decided to trade these smaller canoes for horses once they reached the Plains Indians.

Private Joseph Whitehouse made a note in his journals that he had made previously about the local Indians who might be "Welch Indians." Both he and John Ordway had heard a popular myth about a tribe of Indians in the West that had descended from an old Welsh trader, recognizable by their strange accent. Ordway thought that perhaps the Flatheads were these so-called Welsh Indians. On the return trip, Whitehouse surmised that the "Cal-apno-wa" Indians they had heard about further up a smaller stream must be the Welsh Indians. He made this assumption because one of the Indians they met on the Columbia told them about these Welsh Indians and that one of them was almost white.[3]

Interesting myths about Native American origins have a long history, so Ordway and Whitehouse were not alone in their interest. As early as 1775, a traveler named James Adair passed through the eastern part of North America, recording American Indian cultures and traditions. He assumed that many of these tribes were descendants of some lost tribes of Israel that had somehow found their way across the Atlantic to settle in North America centuries before.[4] In the mid-nineteenth century, the founder of the Mormon faith, Joseph Smith, claimed there was evidence to support this belief in the Book of Mormon. Adair and others believed that similarities in some of the native ceremonies to Jewish ones helped prove the connection. Ordway and Whitehouse were not able to verify that they had found Native Americans who had descended from Europeans, but others found this idea intriguing when they later read their journals of the expedition.

Whether or not the Indians they were meeting during this part of the trip had any European ancestry, they were certainly less friendly than those near the ocean with whom they had traded all winter. Game was scarce here in the early spring, and many of the Indians they met were hungry and afraid that the white men would take their food. While Clark was exploring a particular village of Indians up a stream, he tried to trade for some wap-too roots. They did not want to trade and acted upset and aggressive toward Clark. Therefore, he tried a little trickery by throwing an artillery fuse into their fire and pulling out his compass with a great show just as the fuse lit and made the fire rise dramatically. The Indians were convinced he had some kind of powerful magic and offered him wap-too, if he would just put out the fire. Of course, the fuse, or port fire match, burned out and the Indians were glad to see him go.[5]

On the return trip, Clark recorded one of the most unusual observations made about American Indians. On April 8, 1806, he wrote that he met an Indian woman who had a blind eye that was very sore, and that many Indians had blindness or eye soreness of some kind. He wrote that he did not know why these Indians seemed to have more eye problems and blindness than other people did, but guessed that it might be caused by sun damage. Since native peoples along the Columbia subsisted primarily on fishing, Clark thought that perhaps the glare of the sun on the river damaged their eyes over time.[6]

A few days later, Lewis complained about a group of Indians that seemed to follow them up the river, crowding around their camp at night. Lewis accused them of stealing several different items, and then some of them ran off with his dog, Seaman. Lewis was so upset about this theft that he ordered some of his men to pursue the natives that had taken his dog, giving them permission to shoot the men if they did not give Seaman up. Some men chased the Indians, who quickly decided to let the dog go and kept running.[7] Lewis was relieved to be reunited with his beloved dog, even though the expedition frequently purchased dogs for food from the Indians. They did so often now on their journey upstream on the Columbia. Elk and other game was simply too scarce to rely on.

One day, as they were attempting to portage around some large falls, they damaged their larger boats, or pirogues. Lewis was not sure they could now manage without purchasing more canoes, and they really needed all their trade goods for food purchases. However, they had no choice, so Lewis sent Clark and some of the others ahead while he took a few men to a nearby village and traded some elk skins for two more canoes and some dogs.[8] Clark recorded that at this point most of their diet consisted of dog meat, and that none of them ever thought twice about eating that meat now. It seemed normal, no longer repulsive, to eat both dog and horse meat when nothing else was available.

On almost every day of April, the journal writers record rain and several days when they could not travel because of the water. Fair mornings often began by bailing out the canoes and reloading the supplies that they had unloaded completely the night before to prevent them from being lost in the river. Sacagawea must have found it a challenge to keep herself and her young toddler Jean-Baptiste dry and healthy during this part of the trip. When they were sometimes grounded by bad weather, the men were busy hunting and attempting to dry the meat over fires. Sacagawea probably spent these days helping to skin carcasses and cutting meat for drying, as well as hunting for roots. She likely taught her young son to help her with some of the simple parts of her tasks. Maybe Toussaint showed Jean-Baptiste his gun and told him stories of bears and the life of a trader.

By the middle of April, the expedition reached the shallow waters near where they would begin their overland ride toward the Missouri River. They were already trying to purchase horses for their journey but were discouraged to find the Indians very unwilling to sell them. Sacagawea showed up in the journals for the first time on the return trip as she accompanied Clark and her husband to find horses to purchase. Sacagawea was probably interpreting sign language or looking for anyone who could speak Shoshone or Mandan, so that she could translate to her husband, who could then communicate with Clark. Even though he was thus able to make his wishes known, these Indians said they needed their horses for hunting and warfare. Clark did manage to buy four horses, and hoped the expedition could get more horses further east. The water was now too shallow for the larger boats, so the expedition abandoned these and journeyed on with only the canoes and a few horses along the shore.[9]

Often along this return journey, many of the natives in the region asked for medicinal help from the white men. They had heard stories about magic medicines that these men had that could cure various kinds of sickness, and some had even experienced these cures from the corps when the expedition had passed through the previous fall. One day, Clark wrote in his journal that he had treated the wife of a chief from whom he was trying to buy more horses. Soon the river would be too shallow for even the canoes, and the only replacement now would be horses. Clark called this chief's wife a "sulky bitch" who must have been really complaining about back and muscle pain. Clark rubbed camphor on her back and covered it with flannel. Apparently, this treatment made the woman feel better right away.[10]

As Lewis and Clark both struggled to barter for horses, they also continued to deal with stealing. At night, the men found they had to sleep with most of their important gear, such as guns, hatchets, knives, and kettles, under their heads or in their arms. Otherwise, much of the next morning might be spent trying to find the missing goods. In some villages, the chief would scold his people when Lewis told him about the thefts during the night. Sometimes these speeches brought the goods back, but often they did not. One night, one of the expensively procured horses disappeared. Apparently, the owner who had sold it had actually lost the horse the previous day in a gambling game. The winner simply came to take his winnings. As they had observed in other villages, the people they now encountered on their way to the mountains loved games of chance and gambled often.[11]

Lewis became so frustrated with the ongoing thefts that one day he finally threatened the Indians and actually beat one who was caught stealing in the camp. Lewis wrote the following about the encounter:

I (am) . . . determined to remain no longer with these villains. They stole another tomahawk from us this morning. . . . I ordered all the spare poles, paddles and the balance of our canoe put on the fire as the morning was cold and also that not a particle should be left for the benefit of the Indians. I detected a fellow in stealing an iron socket of a canoe pole and gave him several severe blows and made the men kick him out of camp. I now informed the Indians that I would shoot the first of them that attempted to steal an article from us . . . that we were not afraid to fight them, that I had it in my power at that moment to kill them all and set fire to their houses, but it was not my wish to treat them with severity provided they would let my property alone.[12]

Lewis was obviously very upset at constantly losing goods and horses that he felt the expedition had traded much too dearly for. It is not surprising that he was worried. He knew they needed to make sure they had enough guns, tools, and other items to get them through the rest of the journey, and they were already running very low on supplies. If the return journey took as long as it had taken to come this far, they would run out of goods to trade.

By the end of April, the expedition had reached the land where the Walla Walla people lived in present-day Washington. They had met them the previous October and had promised to stop and trade with them again. Chief Yellepet was very happy to see them and began trading, inviting them to stay an extra night, which they did.[13] While they were trading for horses and extra food (mostly dogs), they found a Shoshone woman prisoner. Since this woman could speak the language of the Walla Walla, Sacagawea was able to communicate Lewis and Clark's wishes to her, and thus to Chief Yellepet. Once again, Sacagawea's translating skills and her ability to speak Shoshone proved a valuable asset. One can also imagine that the two Shoshone women had much to share with each other about their experiences as prisoners.

## CLARK, THE TRAVELING DOCTOR

As they had been on the outbound journey, Clark's medicines were very popular among the Indians they visited. While he was with the Walla Walla, Clark treated several of these native people with sore eyes, one with a broken arm, and one with rheumatism. Clark again wrote in his journal that perhaps the eye problem, which seemed very common among the Walla Walla, was caused by bright sunlight shining on the river. These Indians fished for salmon as their primary means of survival, and Clark thought the light on the water had damaged their eyes in some way.[14]

As they traveled west and left the Walla Walla behind, they encountered the Nez Perce again. This time, the Nez Perce were friendly right from the start since they recognized the travelers. Some of them also had eye problems and remembered that Clark had given eye medicines to the people when he was last among them. Clark treated a prominent leader of the village they visited on May 5. The previous fall, Clark had treated a Nez Perce man for sore muscles in the knee and thigh. Apparently, whatever he gave the man had worked very well, or at least the man recovered. He was so pleased that he talked of little else for a very long time. By the time the Lewis and Clark expedition came through their valley the following year, many Nez Perce were ready to be similarly healed by Clark.[15] He had also aided another man the preceding fall who had a boil, which Clark lanced and cleansed. This man also spread the news of Clark's so-called magic.

As the ill and wounded of the Nez Perce flocked around the expedition's camp, Clark began treating all kinds of ailments the best way he knew how. Those who came for treatment also brought items to trade for their medicine, even horses. Clark wrote in his journal that he decided to play upon this perception and administer "medicines" to whoever asked, even when he did not have cures:

> Those two cures has raised my reputation and given those natives an exalted opinion of my skill as a phician [sic]. I have already received many applications. In our present situation, I think it pardonable to continue this deception for they will not give us any provisions without compensation . . . and our stock is now reduced to a mere handful.[16]

He also wrote that he always made sure he never gave anything that would hurt the people who came for help, and that in fact he sometimes had real treatments for them.

Even though Clark was considered a healer of some sort, the Nez Perce did not think very highly of the expedition's eating habits. One Nez Perce derided them for eating dogs, which they purchased from the Indians any chance they had.[17] They were finding very little game through the plains in which they now traveled, so they resorted to eating dogs and sometimes horses. They had done so at numerous times during the journey already, so they had long since lost any revulsion they might have had about eating them. The Indians, however, did not understand their need for red meat. They offered bread made of pounded roots, but this food seemed much too meager to the men. The members of the expedition had also not been much inclined toward eating fish until that seemed to be the only alternative.

Before leaving the Nez Perce, Clark again treated a large number of people with sore eyes and a small girl who had rheumatism. It is not clear what illness the child actually had, and today, the term *rheumatism* is generally not used. At the time, however, it was often used to describe arthritis and a host of other inflammatory disorders. Clark bathed her in warm water and then rubbed her down with something he called "Balsom Capivia."[18] This ointment was made from the resin or sap taken from the Copaiba, a South American tree. It has apparently been used since the 1600s by herbal practitioners to treat everything from digestive problems to excess mucus and to encourage blood clotting. It is still available today from herbal remedy shops.

Perhaps because of Clark's reputation as a healer, the expedition's encounters with Indians were now very pleasant and amiable. At each village, they found the people helpful and willing to trade for medicinal treatment. At one point on the trail, some Indians brought them two containers of gunpowder that the expedition had buried the previous fall. The Indians had found the powder when they saw that animals had dug up the containers. They carefully protected the powder and then returned it to the men when they came through again. Some of the men wrote in their journals about how honest and helpful these Indians seemed to be. Patrick Gass wrote the following assessment:

> All the Indians from the Rocky Mountains to the falls of the Columbia are an honest, ingenuous and well disposed people; but from the falls to the seacoast, and along it, they are a rascally, thieving set.[19]

Lewis recorded similar sentiments in his journals. Clark's medicines probably helped create some of this good will.

Clark later wrote of another ailment he saw among the Nez Perce, paralysis of limbs. While it was not common, like the sore eyes, Clark saw several cases and found it interesting and puzzling. At one village, a chief was brought to him for treatment who had been unable to use his arms and legs for over five years. He was otherwise perfectly healthy, ate well, and was of sound mind. Clark found the condition very strange and tried to make him comfortable, but had no cure for this paralysis. He surmised that it might be caused by the poor diet of vegetables they relied on for so much of the year. Clark simply could not conceive of a healthy person who did not eat red meat on a regular basis.[20]

For the next month, the Corps of Discovery lived among the Nez Perce. They had not intended to stay so long, but when they had arrived, the Nez Perce told them that there was still too much snow on the mountains to make their crossing. While they waited for the snow to melt, Clark kept very busy doctoring the sick while Lewis and the rest of the men hunted and rounded up the horses they had left there the previous fall. One day, Clark recorded that he had treated at least 40 people for sore eyes. Lewis wrote that it was nearly 50.[21]

On May 16, both Lewis and Clark wrote in their journals that Sacagawea had been gathering roots and wild onions. In this land of the Nez Perce, she found much more in the way of wild roots and herbs than she had further west. Lewis wrote very appreciatively of the fennel roots Sacagawea gathered, declaring that they tasted like anis seed. He further elaborated that this root seemed to be a good antidote to the side effects of eating some of the other common roots he called cows root and quawmash. Apparently, eating the latter roots caused gas, and Lewis stated that eating the fennel roots helped "dispel the wind" and tasted good. Clark wrote that the fennel root was "paleatiable [sic] and nourishing [sic] food."[22]

These roots were so flavorful that Sacagawea began gathering large quantities of them and drying them out for storage. She planned to supplement the group's diet on their mountain crossing and wanted to make sure she had enough to get them through lean times. It must have also been important to her to make sure her young son Jean-Baptiste had enough to eat. She did not want him to go hungry, as the rest of the corps had done on a regular basis on the journey. Clark continued to treat sick people who came to him for help. Sacagawea would gather food and translate when she was needed.[23]

At least for a few moments, Lewis contemplated having his men gather roots with Sacagawea in order to have enough for the mountain journey. There was another root, however, that was very poisonous and looked very much like the cows root. Lewis thus decided to keep the men busy doing other things so that they would not accidentally poison themselves and the rest of the expedition. Instead, he sent them to trade for roots and bread from the Nez Perce with whatever they had left to barter. In most cases, all they had were a few needles, ribbons, and other very small trinkets. They did manage to return with a large amount of dried roots, which added to what Sacagawea had gathered.

A serious problem now arose for Clark's doctoring skills. Jean-Baptiste had become ill with some kind of mysterious ailment. His jaw and throat swelled up, followed by a high fever. Clark treated him with "a poultice of onions" and gave him cream of tartar and other medicines. Cream of tartar was often used in this period as a laxative. Lewis wrote that the child was "cutting teeth."[24] It might be that he developed what today might be a simple childhood illness, but in the early nineteenth century, even common childhood ailments could be fatal.

For the first several days of treatment, little Jean-Baptiste did not improve very much. Clark seemed to be trying to purge him by giving him the cream of tartar. Lewis reported the day after the first treatment that this substance had "worked" on him several times. His neck remained swollen, however, and they kept putting on fresh onion poultices. His fever did break after the third day, but the swelling increased, worrying the men. Sacagawea must have been very concerned for her child. While losing children before the age of two was a very common occurrence, it was always a difficult experience, and Jean-Baptiste was Sacagawea's first child. She was also very young and must have felt helpless and frightened for her boy.

Clark could not devote all his time to tending to the little boy, however. One of the men of the party, William Bratton, was also very ill. He had felt bad for days, and although he could eat just fine, he could barely sit up, much less walk, without severe pain. His muscles ached and were very weak. It is not at all clear what was ailing Bratton, but another member of the expedition, John Shields, now became something of a doctor himself. He told Clark that he had heard that similar ailments could be sweated out of a person and that drinking a tea made from snakeroot while sweating would help. So, the men dug a hole, lined it with stones, and built a fire in the bottom. Once the fire had burned very hot and the stones had been heated, they took the fire out and had Bratton sit down in the hole. They then covered the top with blankets to hold in the heat and had Bratton sprinkle the stones inside with a little cool water, thus making steam. After sweating in this makeshift sauna and sipping snakeroot tea, Bratton rested well and felt almost completely normal the next day.[25]

Since the experiment had gone so well, Clark tried the same approach with the old chief who had been paralyzed for five years. His men had brought him back to the expedition's camp, hoping for some kind of a cure. Unfortunately, the man had not improved with the previous treatment and Lewis thought that perhaps he might benefit from electric shocks. It is interesting to see such a reference in the journals, written in 1806. At this time, scientists had managed to create an instrument that could produce and maintain an electrical current. To know about the use of such instruments in medical treatment was remarkable for a man like Meriwether Lewis. However, since they had no such instrument, they tried sweating instead. Since the man could not sit up, they could not use the sweating pit they had made for Bratton and gave instructions to the chief's men on how to make a sweathouse and give him treatments back in his village.[26]

Finally, about a week after he first became ill, little Jean-Baptiste showed signs of improvement. His fever abated, and the swelling began to decrease in his neck. Both Lewis and Clark wrote about his getting better and sounded very relieved. The little boy, now about fifteen months old, was a mascot of the Corps of Discovery. Clark had developed a great fondness for the boy, and no one wanted to see Sacagawea, their faithful translator and gatherer of good roots, suffer the loss of her child. So far, they had only suffered one casualty among their expedition early in the journey. Both Lewis and Clark continued to keep a close eye on the boy, and Clark kept applying poultices and giving the boy a variety of medicines from his stores.

A few days later, the chief with paralyzed limbs was brought back to the camp and requested they find a way to give him the sweating treatment. So the men made their makeshift sauna larger, and the chief's father went into the hole with him to help him sit up. After the sweat, he felt weak, but after a few more treatments, the man actually began regaining the use of his limbs. Both Lewis and Clark were pleasantly surprised by this development. They hoped that more sweats might actually restore the man to perfect health.[27] Clark's reputation as a healer no doubt increased after the experience with the paralyzed chief. Since he had been unable to use his limbs for five years, such a sudden recovery must have seemed like a work of magic to the Nez Perce.

## MOUNTAIN CROSSING

As the weeks passed, Lewis thought more and more about the difficult crossing they were about to make over the Rocky Mountains. On June 2, he wrote the following:

> McNeal and York were sent on a trading voyage over the river this morning . . . in order to prepare in the most ample manner in our power to meet that wretched portion of our journey, the Rocky Mountain, where hunger and cold in their most rigorous forms assail the wearied traveler; not any of us have yet

forgotten our sufferings in those mountains in September last, and I think it probable we never shall.[28]

No matter how much they prepared and how many roots Sacagawea gathered, they were all concerned. The journey east over the mountains had been very difficult and took much longer than predicted. Sacagawea must have also worried about the health of her young son during such a crossing, especially since he was just recovering from illness.

There was, however, only so much they could do to prepare for the crossing. They had purchased and gathered up horses, and they had stored numerous bushels of various roots and dried meat and bread that they had managed to trade for and preserve. They had traded almost all of the goods that they could spare. Now they simply waited for the snow to finish melting. They knew it would soon be time to move again as they watched the water in the river rise a little each day from snowmelt in the mountains. The Nez Perce were beginning to harvest salmon as the spring run finally began, bringing some variety to their sparse diet. The expedition even fished, although they continued to prefer red meat, even if it was horse meat.

Although several weeks had now passed, Sacagawea's son was still under close supervision by Clark. While the swelling had finally gone, there was still a small boil that Clark watched carefully. He changed his treatment from onion poultices to a salve made from tree resin, bear oil, and beeswax.[29] He must have hoped this ointment would continue to make the boil decrease in size and disappear. Meanwhile, some of the Indians told Lewis that the expedition should not cross the mountains until the middle of July. If they went earlier, there would be no grass for their horses for two or three days near the top. Lewis found this news distressing, but concluded they would not be able to wait that long regardless of the risk.

Finally, on June 10, they set out from their camp with the Nez Perce toward the Rocky Mountains. They moved slowly at first, hunting and gathering more roots before they reached higher ground. Lewis was anxious about the journey but just as eager to be moving. As they began this difficult section of the return trip, Lewis wrote the following:

> We have now been detained near five weeks in consequence of the snows; a serious loss of time at this delightful season for traveling. I am still apprehensive that the snow and the want of food for our horses will prove a serious embarrassment to us as at least four days journey of our route in these mountains lies over heights and along a ledge of mountains never entirely

destitute of snow. Everybody seems anxious to be in motion, convinced that we have not now any time to delay if the calculation is to reach the United States this season; this I am determined to accomplish if within the compass of human power.[30]

If Sacagawea was concerned about the journey, no one made a note of it in the journals. However, she had already managed many obstacles, while carrying a very young baby on her back. She was probably eager to return to Shoshone lands to see her brother.

Difficulties began even before they reached the high ground. First, Lewis sent some men back to the Nez Perce to try to convince some of them to serve as guides over the mountains. They were already encountering snow at least eight feet deep, but still frozen hard enough on top to allow both men and horses to walk on its crust without falling through. One man, however, accidentally cut his leg with a hunting knife, severing a large artery. Lewis struggled to stop the bleeding, eventually applying a type of tourniquet before it stopped. The man could easily have died from such a wound if it had not been for Lewis's fast thinking.

The next day, Lewis decided that they had to turn back a day's journey to a lower area while they waited for the return of the men sent to find Indian guides. There was very little game where they now camped, and the hunters would not be able to feed the corps if they stayed there waiting for the return of the men. Lewis did not like retracing his steps, but saw no other solution. They went back a day's journey and began hunting and storing up food as best they could. After two days, the men finally returned with Indian guides, and the Corps of Discovery moved forward again. Soon, Sacagawea found a familiar plant that the Shoshones often ate—a small root that Lewis and Clark described in their journals as similar to a Jerusalem artichoke.

Once again, Sacagawea proved her worth to the party, providing variety to their meager diet. The plant she found was also very interesting to the expedition as a new species that they had not noticed themselves. Her addition of this plant was carefully placed in their specimen collection of new discoveries. Sacagawea was now truly a full-fledged member of the expedition as a collector of specimens.[31]

After four days, the expedition made it over the mountains. The journey went much more smoothly than anyone had anticipated, and although they had worried about their horses, the men and Sacagawea had plenty of roots to eat. The mountain crossing had been much shorter than the way they had journeyed through the previous year, and everyone was relieved to have had guides to help them. Once they reached the bottom, the horses found plenty of grass on which to graze, and the men even found a hot springs they could take a bath in.[32] Although the journals do not say if Sacagawea enjoyed the hot springs, one can imagine that she must have. Few would have passed up such an opportunity.

Now that they were over the mountains, Lewis and Clark decided to take separate paths back toward the Mandan villages. Clark would take Sacagawea, her husband and son, and most of the men with him on as direct a route as possible back to the Mandans. Lewis would take six men and explore up the Marias River. They soon parted ways and hoped that all would go well. A few days after they divided, Sacagawea recognized a valley through which they were passing. She pointed out to Clark a gap in the mountains through which they should pass in order to find the canoes they had left there the previous year.[33]

Although later writers would use this incident as an example to argue that Sacagawea had been a guide for the expedition, this entry and a few more later that week, are the only ones that really refer to any guidance she gave them. Sacagawea had recognized Shoshone country on the way east and had been able to reassure Lewis and Clark that they would find her people soon. Now on the return journey, she again recognized land she had known as a child. She was then able to briefly point out a pathway through the mountain gap for Clark. On the rest of the journey, Sacagawea served only in the capacity of translator and gatherer of roots and plants, according to the records. It is a romantic view that this American Indian woman served as a guide to the white people, but in truth, her contribution was not as a guide. There were plenty of times, no doubt, that Sacagawea herself must have wondered if they would ever find their way back to the Mandan villages that had become her home.

A few days after Sacagawea first recognized the valley, she again brought a new plant to Clark's attention. The plant had a root that looked and tasted much like a carrot, although paler in color.[34] She also recognized a pass that she advised Clark to take as they continued east. What is now called Bozeman Pass was a pathway through the mountains that Sacagawea recognized from her childhood journeys. Clark trusted Sacagawea's judgment and wrote, "The Indian woman who has been of great service to me as a pilot through this country recommends a gap in the mountain more South which I shall cross."[35] Only in this familiar country did Sacagawea give advice on which direction to travel in. Clark, however, was very grateful for her knowledge of the region and followed her suggestion.

Soon they came to a low plain where Sacagawea pointed out an old buffalo road. She told Clark that her people used to follow this road to hunt for buffalo when they needed hides. If he followed this road, he would arrive at the gap that she had suggested he take through the mountains. Clark again followed her advice and followed the buffalo path.[36] A day or two later, the party encountered a fort built of logs and bark. Sacagawea told Clark that her people sometimes built these forts to defend themselves from the Crows who frequently attacked them. Since the Crows outnumbered the Shoshones, they found these small forts a good defense against superior numbers.

On July 25, Clark came upon what he called a very large rock resting beside a creek. It was probably about 200 feet high, and Clark climbed it to get a better view of the lay of the land. He decided to name this landmark Pompy's Tower.[37] Pompy or Little Pomp was Clark's nickname for little Jean-Baptiste. Lewis and Clark had the habit all throughout their expedition of naming mountains, streams, and other natural features after members of their party, presidents, and other important people including Sacagawea and her husband Toussaint. Now even their young son had his name, or at least his nickname, memorialized. No doubt, Clark was becoming very fond of Jean-Baptiste. The degree of his fondness would become evident after the journey had ended.

While Clark journeyed to the mouth of the Yellowstone River with Sacagawea, Toussaint, and Little Pomp, Lewis and his men ended up in a brief skirmish with some Crow Indians, during which two were killed. Lewis felt upset about this event, the only time on the entire journey when they fired upon and killed American Indians to whom they were serving as ambassadors. Ironically, Lewis was shot by accident a few days later by one of his own men when they were hunting. Thankfully, the wound was not serious, only very uncomfortable.

On August 12, Lewis and Clark reunited on the river and traveled swiftly downstream, reaching the Hidatsa villages on August 14 and then arriving at Fort Mandan. On August 17, the journey was all over for Sacagawea. Clark paid Toussaint for his services as interpreter and said goodbye to Sacagawea and little Jean-Baptiste. Even though her contributions to the expedition had been significant, there was no pay for her. Clark was very reluctant to leave Little Pomp. He offered to take the child with him to raise and educate him. He was about 19 months old at this point and not yet weaned. Therefore, Toussaint told Clark that he would bring the child to him in St. Louis perhaps in about a year.

One wonders how Sacagawea felt about this arrangement. In both her native culture, and certainly in both English and French culture, the father had full control over the future of his children. At least for now, the decision was made, and Clark waved good-bye to Sacagawea and her son, his two constant companions on his historic journey to the Pacific.

Sacagawea must have felt mixed emotions as she watched the Corps of Discovery head downstream. She must have been very glad to be finished with the hardships of travel. She must also have been happy to return to some degree of normal life as wife and mother. Yet, she must also have felt sadness, for Clark had been an important figure in her life for the better part of the last two years. She would see him again in a few years.

## NOTES

1. John Ordway and Patrick Gass, March 30, 1806, in *The Journals of the Lewis and Clark Expedition*, ed. Gary E. Moulton (Lincoln: University of Nebraska Press, 1983–2001). Also made available online by University of Nebraska Press at http://lewisandclarkjournals.unl.edu/index.html. Listed hereafter as *JLC*.

2. Gass, March 28, 1806, *JLC*.

3. Joseph Whitehouse, April 2, 1806, *JLC*.

4. James Adair, *History of the American Indians* (1775; New York: Promontory Press, 1930).

5. William Clark, April 6, 1806, *JLC*.

6. Clark, April 8, 1806, *JLC*.

7. Meriwether Lewis, April 11, 1806, *JLC*.

8. Clark, April 12, 1806, *JLC*.

9. Clark, April 16 and 19, 1806, *JLC*.

10. Clark, April 18, 1806, *JLC*.

11. Ordway, April 20, 1806, *JLC*.

12. Lewis, April 21–22, 1806, *JLC*.

13. Clark, April 28, 1806, *JLC*.

14. Ibid.

15. Clark, May 5, 1806, *JLC*.

16. Ibid.

17. Ordway, May 5, 1808, *JLC*.

18. Clark, May 6, 1806, *JLC*.

19. Gass, May 7, 1806, *JLC*.

20. Clark, May 11, 1806, *JLC*.

21. Lewis and Clark, May 12, 1806, *JLC*.

22. Lewis and Clark, May 16, 1806, *JLC*.

23. Clark, May 18, 1806, *JLC*.

24. Lewis and Clark, May 21, 1806, *JLC*.

25. Lewis, May 24, 1806, *JLC*.

26. Lewis and Clark, May 25, 1806, *JLC*.

27. Clark, May 30, 1806, *JLC*.

28. Lewis, June 2, 1806, *JLC*.

29. Clark, June 5, 1806, *JLC*.

30. Lewis, June 14, 1806, *JLC*.

31. Lewis, June 25, 1806, and footnote 1, *JLC*.

32. Harold P. Howard, *Sacagawea* (Norman: University of Oklahoma Press, 1971), 110.

33. Clark, July 6, 1806, *JLC*.

34. Clark, July 9, 1806, *JLC*.

35. Clark, July 13, 1806. *JLC*.

36. Clark, July 14, 1806, *JLC*.

37. Clark, July 25, 1806, *JLC*.

# Chapter 8

# AFTER THE JOURNEY

With the most famous part of their lives over, the various members of the Corps of Discovery would go on to live more normal lives. Most of the enlisted men disappeared, leaving no records behind of what came next for them. Perhaps some of them became famous in their local areas; most likely many returned to a very ordinary sort of existence. The officers went on to more interesting affairs. Some would return to the frontier and Indian country; others would serve in government or military posts. President Thomas Jefferson appointed Meriwether Lewis governor of the new Louisiana Territory that he and his friend William Clark had helped claim and explore. Lewis would be dead in 1809, just three years after his triumphal return from the West.

There is still controversy surrounding his death. It appeared to be a suicide, and indeed, Lewis had collected a lot of debt in the few years after the expedition. Others thought there might be some evidence of murder. Unfortunately, we may never know for certain, but most scholars lean toward evidence of suicide. Lewis was a melancholy person, far behind in his debts, and had made no real progress in revising the expedition journals he was supposed to publish. His task as governor of such a large territory was probably overwhelming, and Lewis missed exploration and adventure.[1] Clark, although he may have also missed the adventure of the trail, lived happily as far as records can reveal. He served as governor of the Missouri Territory and as a government agent to the American Indians west of the Mississippi.

## SACAGAWEA'S DEATH

It must have been a bittersweet parting at Fort Mandan when the expedition finally arrived in August 1806. As the rest of the corps sailed downstream to St. Louis, Sacagawea and Toussaint must have had mixed emotions. Clark had been their constant companion and had developed a great fondness for little Jean-Baptiste, whom he had offered to educate in St. Louis. The parents knew this was a generous offer but decided that Little Pomp was still too young, and they were unwilling to travel with Clark to St. Louis at that time. Three years later, in 1809, they did decide to accept Clark's offer, and for a time, they tried a more settled life, farming some nearby land. This arrangement did not last very long, however, and soon Toussaint wanted to head back into the wilderness that he knew and loved.

Apparently, Sacagawea also missed her home and decided to go with her husband on the trail in 1811, leaving Jean-Baptiste in Clark's care. It is hard to imagine being able to leave a young child behind, and perhaps Sacagawea did not intend the arrangement to be permanent. It is quite possible that she thought her good friend could provide more of a future for Jean-Baptiste and that she would visit often. She may not have seen her son again. The records do show that she became pregnant again and gave birth to a daughter, Lizette, in 1812. That same year, Toussaint once again accompanied a fur-trading expedition, and Sacagawea went along with her daughter. She was not feeling at all well and might have been hoping to see her people once again.

One of the people along for the journey in 1812 was John C. Luttig. He was a St. Louis businessman, apparently seeking some change in his life. The expedition stopped just below the North Dakota border in present-day South Dakota on the banks of the Missouri River and built a fort they called Fort Manuel. Mr. Luttig stayed at the fort and worked as a clerk, keeping records of all the comings and goings until the company abandoned the fort the following year. His almost daily journal entries provide the only real evidence concerning the end of Sacagawea's life. The records do seem clear that she traveled with Toussaint in 1811 and again in 1812 as far as Fort Manuel. Luttig recorded the presence of Charbonneau at the fort during this period in a few brief entries, and then on December 20, he recorded the following:

> This evening the wife of Charbonneau, a Snake squaw, died of a putrid fever. She was a good and the best woman in the fort, aged about 25 years. She left a fine infant girl.[2]

There are no other records, and most historians today agree that this journal entry clearly referred to Sacagawea. Thus, evidence suggests that she never saw Jean-Baptiste again, and soon after, Clark received legal guardianship of both Jean-Baptiste and Lizette.

She had lived a very short life and only survived for a few years after the expedition to the Pacific Ocean. What her life might have been had she lived, one will never know. Perhaps she would have taken her son back to Mandan or Shoshone country in a few years, or maybe she would have decided to settle near him in St. Louis. Maybe she planned regular visits but intended to continue her journeys on the trail as long as her husband worked in that capacity. She must have enjoyed the wilderness as much as her husband did to be willing to make a difficult journey again just five years after the Lewis and Clark Expedition. If she had lived, she might have been known as a great trailblazer, just as her husband and son were. As a woman, however, she might have always stayed in the shadows. Perhaps because she died so young, her role on the famous Lewis and Clark expedition has been romanticized in literature and film to the present day. While her husband and son have been nearly forgotten, Sacagawea has become a national symbol, surrounded by more myth than fact.

## TOUSSAINT CHARBONNEAU

What became of Toussaint Charbonneau after the Lewis and Clark expedition? As far as historians know, Charbonneau continued to work for the Mandans as an interpreter, but then accepted Clark's offer to go to St. Louis in 1809. By this time, his young son Jean-Baptiste would have been about five or six years old and ready for the education that Clark had promised to provide. Toussaint bought some land and tried farming, but only for a few months. Very soon, he found he did not like the farming life and sold his land back. He found another trading expedition going west that needed an interpreter and continued to serve in this capacity for the rest of his recorded life. At first, Sacagawea went with him, but after her death in 1812, Toussaint journeyed without her wherever he could find someone to pay him for his services.

Shortly after Sacagawea's death, Charbonneau hatched a money-making plan with a trapper named Edward Rose. They traveled west to Arapaho country and purchased from the Arapahos a number of female Shoshone captives. They then sold these captives as wives to trappers on the Missouri River. It is ironic that their plan involved something similar to the way that Toussaint had gained Sacagawea as a wife years before.

Apparently, he did not take one of these women as a wife but did make some money on the deal.[3] Perhaps actions like this helped Charbonneau develop a reputation as a rogue and womanizer.

As the years passed, however, Charbonneau showed up in journal accounts as a good interpreter and an excellent trail cook. No one would remember him as a good equestrian or boatman. Apparently, Lewis and Clark's assessment of him remained accurate later in life. Yet, while Lewis had only criticism of the Frenchman after the expedition was over, Clark tried to help Charbonneau and his family as much as he could. When Charbonneau gave up on farming and returned to the trail, he and Sacagawea left their young son in Clark's care. He continued translating for the Mandans and perhaps settled more permanently with them in his later years.

In 1839, Joshua Pilcher, the Indian agent in Missouri, wrote of seeing Charbonneau in the Mandan villages and paying him for his services. Pilcher also told him the government would no longer need him, so at the age of approximately 72, Charbonneau was retired from service. During the last 30 years of his life, he frequently appeared in the journals of trappers throughout the Missouri River valley region. Even at his ripe age, he never lost his interest in women. He apparently married his last wife, a 14-year-old American Indian captive he had purchased, in 1839. It is not known exactly when or where Charbonneau died. It is possible he lived well into his eighties, although such a long life was rare for the period. The only evidence is the legal execution of a will in 1843, giving money to Jean-Baptiste from his father's estate.[4]

One of the sad events we can at least speculate about occurred in 1837 when a smallpox epidemic struck the Mandan people. Charbonneau likely watched many of his friends die, and survivors might have blamed him for the outbreak. Of course, the white man's arrival had brought the disease to people who had no immunity to it. Many natives believed that the whites had caused the painful and fatal disease on purpose in order to take their lands. Charbonneau probably had to flee the region, since he, too, was a white man. It is likely, however, that Charbonneau simply took up residence with other Indians, perhaps farther west, and lived out the end of his life there. We will never know for sure.

## THE DANCING BOY

We know more about what happened later in life to Little Pomp, or Jean-Baptiste Charbonneau. He must have enjoyed his very young years, growing older and learning to walk and run among other Mandan children. His childhood might have been much like many other American Indian children his age if his parents had not taken such an extraordinary journey to the West.

He no doubt grew up hearing stories from his mother and father about the Corps of Discovery, their struggles through rapids and falls, rocky mountain crossings, and difficult portages. He must have heard them talk about seeing the Pacific Ocean, the carcass of a whale, and meeting many other native people. When they finally took him down the Missouri River to St. Louis, he must have been excited. He would not remember Clark from the journey, but had heard many stories about the man who called him Little Pomp. He might also have been frightened to see such a large city.

Apparently, the six-year-old boy and Clark got along very well because when Toussaint gave up on farming three months after arriving in St. Louis, he and Sacagawea left Jean-Baptiste in St. Louis. Clark had promised to raise and educate the boy, probably thinking this might be the best way he could ever adequately compensate Toussaint and Sacagawea for their services on the expedition. He kept his word and took the little boy in as his own child. Records show he spent money on tutors and books for young Jean-Baptiste, whom Clark had referred to lovingly as the Dancing Boy on more than one occasion.

Probably very soon after their arrival in St. Louis, Toussaint arranged for a proper Catholic baptism for young Jean-Baptiste. There is no evidence that Charbonneau had much of a religious practice, but he wanted to do what he thought was right for his young son's eternal salvation. One wonders what Sacagawea thought about the baptism or if she was at all interested in this religion of the white people. There is no evidence to suggest that she converted to Christianity during her short life, but nothing to indicate that she objected to it. As many of her people had done upon the arrival of French Jesuit missionaries, she might have found it comfortable to have two sets of religious practices to follow, one traditional and one Christian. Perhaps this is also how Jean-Baptiste handled religion in his life, although we have no evidence.

Regardless, Jean-Baptiste was soon immersed in the white, European world that would have included Christianity. He had to continue learning both English and French in order to fit into Clark's life in St. Louis. He had to learn proper manners and to communicate with other students in school who might taunt him for being a "half-breed" or a "wild savage." Jean-Baptiste probably tried very hard to become as much like the other children around him as quickly as possible in order to both please Clark and fit in with others.

On top of all these adjustments, Jean-Baptiste had to learn how to live without his parents, especially his mother Sacagawea who had so dutifully and carefully carried him as an infant on her back all the way to the Pacific Ocean. One wonders if they thought they would all see each other again—the father, mother, and young son of about six years old. Jean-Baptiste probably saw his father again when Toussaint traveled to St. Louis in 1812 to join another fur-trading expedition. Perhaps Sacagawea came with him. However, since there is no record, it is possible that she did not since she was pregnant.[5] Nevertheless, Sacagawea died in December of 1812 at Fort Manuel in present-day South Dakota, leaving behind another young child, an infant daughter named Lizette. Probably because Toussaint could not think of a better caregiver for his children while he trekked the wilderness, he granted Clark full custody of Jean-Baptiste and of one-year-old Lizette in 1813.[6]

It must have been comforting for young Jean-Baptiste to have a little sister to come home to after school. There are no surviving records of Lizette's life after 1813. Jean-Baptiste, however, must have done well in school and grown up with excellent skills in English. A private tutor educated him for the first several years with Clark, as there were no public schools in St. Louis in the early nineteenth century. When he was 13, however, Clark sent him to a Catholic school called St. Louis Academy. At this school, Jean-Baptiste studied a traditional curriculum that emphasized languages such as Greek, Latin, English, French, Spanish, and Italian, as well as mathematics, drawing, and geography.[7] In fact, Jean-Baptiste would later add more languages to his list. There are no records of how well Jean-Baptiste did in school, but he must have done well enough because Clark continued paying tuition for this private school and purchasing various schoolbooks and other supplies that he needed. Clark's records of purchases from 1820 list a "Roman history, Scott's Lessons, one dictionary, slate and pencils, paper and quills."[8]

When he was about 15 years old, Jean-Baptiste experienced the loss of another parental figure, Clark's young wife Julia. Clark soon remarried, but his second wife also died very young in 1831. Jean-Baptiste was a young adult by then, but so many losses must have affected him. Certainly, these losses and the deaths of two of Clark's sons must have been hard. When Jean-Baptiste was 18 or so, Clark permitted him to go work for the Missouri Fur Company. Jean-Baptiste probably longed to follow his father's example and to live in the wilderness as his mother's people did. This might have troubled Clark, since he had spent so much time and money educating the young man. By the time he was 18, Jean-Baptiste could probably speak at least five languages, if not more, and could have worked at any number of professions. The tragedies at home, however, might have persuaded Clark to allow Jean-Baptiste to get out of the city and see the world.

While Jean-Baptiste he was so employed, he met an interesting person who would influence his future. His name was Friedrich Paul Wilhelm, Duke of Württemberg, directly related to the king of Württemberg as well as the czar of Russia and other European royals. As was typical of wealthy young men at the time, especially those of royal descent who would not be directly inheriting a throne, Friedrich Paul Wilhelm traveled the world and decided that the frontier city of St. Louis in the United States was an important destination. Thus, in 1823 at the age of 25, Duke Wilhelm arrived in St. Louis and soon met Jean-Baptiste. The duke wanted to travel along the Mississippi, Missouri, and Columbia rivers to see the vast western wilderness.

Perhaps at the instigation of Clark himself, Duke Wilhelm and Jean-Baptiste met and instantly liked each other. After some journeys into the western wilderness, the duke returned with a plan to take Jean-Baptiste back to Germany with him for more education. Clark agreed to this plan, and Jean-Baptiste spent the next five and a half years in Europe under the guardianship of the duke. Clark must have had great confidence in Jean-Baptiste's ability to handle himself as a mature adult at the age of 18 and must have hoped that he would learn even more language skills that would serve him well in the future. Jean-Baptiste must have seen the trip as another journey into the frontier, albeit an old and settled one. Truly, such a journey was an amazing event for a young man born of a Shoshone mother among the Mandan people.

Not much is known about his years in Germany with the duke. He did apparently develop a love interest and had a child by a woman named Anastasia Katharina Fries. The child died at only three months old, but Jean-Baptiste might have already been on his way back home to St. Louis when the death occurred in 1829.[9] In any case, Jean-Baptiste returned home in December with the duke, ready for more journeys into the wilderness. For the next two years, Jean-Baptiste and the duke traveled with fur-trading companies along the Missouri. At some point, Jean-Baptiste left the duke and worked in the Rubidoux Fur Brigade starting probably in 1830. Duke Wilhelm remained in the United States for another two years, but there are no records of whether the two men spent any more time together. Jean-Baptiste was now truly a man and on his own, working in the fur-trade business as his father had done.

By the time Jean-Baptiste entered the fur trade again in 1830, life in the business had gotten tougher, and the competition was strong. In many ways, the Lewis and Clark expedition at the beginning of the century had opened up the trans-Mississippi west to many people. Fur traders in particular sought a piece of the lucrative trade with the American Indians that the French had controlled up to that time. Jean-Baptiste had a real advantage in the trade since he spoke so many languages. Still, the job was a risky one, with the constant threat of dangerous terrain, lack of supplies, and attack by Indians. While some of these years are sketchy, there are records of Jean-Baptiste in the journals of other trappers in the West. In 1832, Jean-Baptiste was in the Rocky Mountain region working as a trapper, perhaps on his own and maybe even teamed up with the famous mountain man Jim Bridger.

As the American Fur Company began to send trappers into the Rockies, competition led to conflict between some of the independent mountain men and these newcomers. At one point in 1832, Jim Bridger was attacked by some other trappers working for the American Fur Company and was hit by two arrows. He luckily survived, and while we do not know for sure if Jean-Baptiste was there for the event, records do show they were working together that same summer. He had his own narrow escape around the same time, when some Indians attacked his group of trappers, stealing their horses and injuring some of the men with arrows. Apparently, Jean-Baptiste was not injured in the scuffle.[10]

A little of Jean-Baptiste's personality appears in some of the records of fur traders who worked with him in the West. In 1834, a man named W. M. Anderson wrote in his diary that Jean-Baptiste had stabbed a man. Apparently, there was some kind of disagreement, and Jean-Baptiste called the man a rogue. In return, the man said that he would like to flog Jean-Baptiste for calling him such a name. This statement inflamed Jean-Baptiste enough to stab the man with a butcher knife in the shoulder muscle, clear up to the hilt.[11] This is an interesting side of Sacagawea's son that is perhaps not terribly unusual for the rough life lived out in the mountains. He might have encountered criticism from other trappers for being a "half-breed" and a "savage." Such treatment was typical for Métis Americans who had one parent of either Native American or African American heritage.

Although there are few records of the next few years, Jean-Baptiste shows up again in diaries in the American Southwest. Moving from the northern Rocky Mountain region as the fur trade began to slow down, Jean-Baptiste again found a way to use his language skills and continue living in the wilderness, exploring and traveling. In the summer of 1839, he ended up at Fort Bent near present-day La Junta, Colorado. It had become a major trading hub for those moving back and forth along the Santa Fe Trail through present-day New Mexico, Arizona, and into Southern

California. Traders along this trail brought Mexican silver, turquoise, and other goods to St. Louis in exchange for guns, ammunition, and other American trade goods. These trading parties needed hunters to feed them, and Jean-Baptiste was employed to hunt.

It is interesting to imagine Jean-Baptiste as both a fur trapper and then a hunter for traders in the Southwest. He obviously had excellent hunting skills in addition to his communication skills, and he must have loved the forests and even the deserts, the open country instead of the urban areas of the East. Yet, Jean-Baptiste was likely the most educated person in any party. He had received an excellent education back in St. Louis and then in Germany, an experience of only the wealthy and highborn at that time. One might think that Clark was disappointed with Jean-Baptiste's career choices. However, evidence suggests that the two kept a close relationship. E. Willard Smith traveled briefly with Jean-Baptiste in 1839 while Smith was moving west with a group of traders. Smith wrote that he had met "Shabenare" who was the son of the famous Captain Clark and that he had been educated in Europe for seven years. The man Smith is describing is certainly Jean-Baptiste.[12]

The interesting thing about this journal entry is that Jean-Baptiste must have identified himself as Clark's son even though Clark was his guardian only. The implication is that the two maintained a good relationship, although we cannot know. Smith did not even question this relationship, even though Jean-Baptiste was obviously part American Indian. Clark must have kept in touch with Jean-Baptiste. Perhaps in Clark, Jean-Baptiste managed to keep the only permanent parental tie he had. Clark must have done far more than just educate Jean-Baptiste. We cannot know for sure, of course, but there is evidence to suggest that they were close.

As the years passed, life in the West changed, and Jean-Baptiste changed with it. When unrest broke out in Texas in 1843, the Santa Fe Trail was closed to traders. Jean-Baptiste found work escorting wealthy and famous visitors on tours of the West. In that year, he helped manage such a tour toward the region that is now Yellowstone for a number of travelers, one of whom was Clark's son Jefferson Kennerly Clark.[13] One of the members of the expedition recorded the irony of the expedition:

> One of the drivers, Baptiste Charbonneau, was the son of the old trapper Charbonneau and Sacajawea, the brave Indian woman who had guided Lewis and Clark on their perilous journey through the wilderness. . . . By a singular coincidence he [Jean-Baptiste] was now again to make the journey and guide the *son* of William Clark through the same region.[14]

Another interesting element to this statement is the picture of Sacagawea as a guide. No wonder the myth developed about her being a guide. American Indian guides were commonly used for trapping expeditions, and this writer already had that image of her.

Before this particular expedition of 1843 was completed, Jean-Baptiste left it, returning to St. Louis to settle his father's affairs. The court records the settlement of Toussaint's estate in that year. Whether he had died recently, or if it had taken a year or so to for the settlement to make it through the courts is not known. Nevertheless, after 1843, Jean-Baptiste no longer had either of his birth parents living. One does wonder how often he might have seen Toussaint, who was himself mostly employed in the frontier as an interpreter. Since men both traveled extensively, they were probably often very far away from each other.

A few years later, Jean-Baptiste worked for the U.S. government in a way he had probably never anticipated. Mostly, he had worked for individuals or fur companies in various capacities. In 1845, he went back to the Southwest for something other than trade. Texas, a province of Mexico, had been settled by American farmers mostly from the Southeast over the previous decade. When Mexico decided to assert tighter control of this region, Texas rebelled and declared independence. Although almost a decade passed before the United States thought it prudent to annex Texas, most people believed it inevitable. The government of Mexico, however, did not want to lose this valuable province but had lost it to the Texan army led by Sam Houston in 1836. In 1845, the United States made moves to annex the province and argued about the boundary. This boundary conflict eventually led to war, which was welcomed by U.S. President James K. Polk. In the process of this war, the United States would annex the entire Southwest and California.

In order to secure the very desirable region of California as a prize of war, President Polk sent Brigadier General Stephen Watts Kearny with an army over the Santa Fe Trail. He was to counter any Mexican forces in that region and declare the territory for the United States. He needed troops, however, and found them hard to obtain for such an expedition west. At this time, the Mormons in Utah were trying hard to counter accusations that they were not loyal Americans. They also wanted the government to approve the building of some winter quarters in Missouri territory for Mormons emigrating west through the harsh wilderness. In exchange, they agreed to provide a battalion to help Kearny on his journey to California.

In July of 1846, Kearny had a Mormon battalion of 497 men, accompanied by 80 women and children who were moving with them to the

West. This party made its famous journey of over two thousand miles and sent a clear statement as it went to anyone thinking of resisting the power of the United States. As the group passed into present-day New Mexico, Kearny worried about his lack of accurate maps. He hired Jean-Baptiste as a guide for the rest of the trip. The expedition journals also mention Jean-Baptiste's skills in Spanish, hunting, and finding water for the horses and mules. Jean-Baptiste would have been in his forties at that point, but he was described as very active, hunting bears and taking risks that others would not. He had lived in the western wilderness for 20 years or more and had an excellent reputation as a tough mountain guide with an uncommon education.

Ironically, much of his work with expeditions, traders, and other travelers was part of what was putting an end to the wilderness he loved. As the West was tamed and settled, there was soon no more need for trail guides or hunters for expeditions. In short, Jean-Baptiste and all the others like him worked themselves out of a job. Whether he was aware of these changes is hard to say. There were still the gold rush wagon trains to come across the West in 1849. These wagon trains, however, traveled on well-established trails and needed no guides, language experts, or hunters.

Perhaps Jean-Baptiste even wanted another job for a while, for soon, he volunteered for a nonpaying position as magistrate for the San Luis Rey Mission. The Mormon battalion had arrived and taken over the mission in 1847, and it housed soldiers to monitor the new territory and its American Indian and Mexican inhabitants. Jean-Baptiste probably thought he could help the local Indians especially, and one of the first things he did was to establish an Indian school. Soon, however, problems arose since Jean-Baptiste did not agree with the governor's policies toward the Indians. He treated them harshly and tried to force them to adopt white ways as quickly as possible. Maybe Jean-Baptiste resisted some of these techniques, because soon he was accused of trying to start an American Indian insurrection. He wrote a letter denying these charges but also spelled out his disagreement with the treatment of the Indians. He argued that giving them liquor at very high prices and paying them so poorly would condemn them to perpetual slavery. No one paid attention to his arguments, and he resigned his post at the mission in the spring of 1848.

Once again, he was riding the trail and headed north toward Sutter's Mill in the Sacramento Valley where just months before, James Marshall had discovered gold. Soon, a rush of gold prospectors would descend upon California, and Jean-Baptiste was caught up in the gold craze. He and some of friends that he met up with in California tried hard to strike it rich, but never did. Instead, he soon collaborated with a friend from his school days in St. Louis to run a hotel in Auburn for miners. They apparently did well with this venture but continued to work claims, panning for gold in their spare time. For the next 18 years, Jean-Baptiste lived a more settled life in California.

As the years passed, Jean-Baptiste found various means to survive. No one knows how long he was in the hotel business with his friend from childhood, but later records show he worked as a surveyor in 1852 and then again as a hotel clerk in 1861. It must have been hard, however, for the wandering mountain man to settle down. California soon filled up with people, became a state in 1850, and continued to draw settlers from all over the globe. Jean-Baptiste must have felt crowded as the years went by; he had never enjoyed urban life. So, when he heard of another gold strike in Montana in 1866, he persuaded a couple of friends to head in that direction. In many ways, he was heading home to the land of his people.

He never arrived. About two weeks after leaving California and before reaching the gold fields, he became ill with pneumonia and died near present-day Danner, Oregon. He was 61 years old and famous in the West. His local newspaper in California, the *Placer Herald*, published a moving obituary that hailed him as a great mountain man, one of the last of his kind.[15] He was remembered fondly by all who knew him and many who had only heard stories about his travels. In so many ways, Jean-Baptiste had lived his life as a legacy to both his French fur-trapper father and his Shoshone mother, Sacagawea.

## NOTES

1. See Larry E. Morris, *The Fate of the Corps: What Became of the Lewis and Clark Explorers after the Expedition* (New Haven: Yale University Press, 2004), 54–74.

2. John C. Luttig, in *Journal of a Fur-Trading Expedition on the Upper Missouri, 1812–1813*, ed. Stella M. Drumm (St. Louis: Missouri Historical Society, 1920). Original manuscript located in the Missouri Historical Society, St. Louis, Missouri.

3. Morris, *The Fate of the Corps*, 134.

4. Ibid., 172.

5. Susan M. Colby, *Sacagawea's Child: The Life and Times of Jean-Baptiste (Pomp) Charbonneau* (Spokane, WA: Arthur H. Clark Company, 2006), 79.

6. Ibid., 90.

7. Ibid., 93.

8. Ibid., 94.

9. Ibid., 111.

10. Ibid., 132.

11. Frederick Taylor, *Pomp: The Long, Adventurous Life of Sacagawea's Son* (Bloomington, IN: AuthorHouse, 2004), 77; and Colby, *Sacagawea's Child*, 137.

12. Colby, *Sacagawea's Child*, 142.

13. Ibid., 150.

14. Ibid., 150–51.

15. July 7, 1866, *Placer Herald* (Placer County Auburn Public Library, Auburn, California).

# Chapter 9

# LEGENDS AND LORE

It all started with an interesting claim made by a Reverend John Roberts of the Shoshone Mission in Wyoming in the early twentieth century. In the years surrounding the first centennial of the Lewis and Clark expedition, people turned their attention to the history of this famous journey and the people involved in it. Sacagawea gained special attention and was proclaimed an important guide for the expedition without whose help the whole enterprise might have been a failure. When a novel about her life was published, centennial organizers, state governors and senators, and even historians began to look for the story of Sacagawea.

## PORIVO AND BA'TIZ

Reverend John Roberts arrived in Wyoming in 1883 with the task of founding the Indian Mission of the Protestant Episcopal Church for the Shoshone and Arapaho tribes. The U.S. agent for these tribes was Dr. James Erwin who immediately introduced Reverend Roberts to a Shoshone named Bazil. After some conversation, Roberts was told that Bazil's mother, a "very old, very old" woman, had accompanied Lewis and Clark on their journey west many years ago.[1] Eventually, Roberts learned that Bazil's mother, or Porivo, as she was called, also had a son named Baptiste, or "Ba'tiz."

Roberts eventually told inquiring historian Grace Raymond Hebard, who was researching Sacagawea, that he truly believed Porivo was Sacagawea. He became friends with Ba'tiz, or the man he presumed to be Jean-Baptiste, son of Sacagawea, and her adopted son Bazil. Porivo died on April 9, 1884, and Roberts presided over her funeral. He claimed that at the time of her death, he did not realize her true significance, but came to learn it later. In his affidavit of 1936 presenting his story to refute retractors, Roberts described some of what he had learned about her before and after her death. He testified that although she never told anyone her name was Sacagawea, she talked about a journey to the Pacific Ocean and seeing a very large fish "as big as a log cabin."[2] Roberts further claimed that after the expedition, Sacagawea (or Porivo) had left her abusive husband, lived with the Comanches for a time, and finally returned to her own people to finish out her days in obscurity.

Such a story was much more appealing to Americans and even scholars than an early death in 1812 at the age of 25. If Sacagawea had lived until old age, then there was more to her story and a place where people could venerate her grave. The state of Wyoming naturally supported the theory that Sacagawea had died in 1884 on the Wind River Reservation. If people believed this theory, many tourists would flock to Wyoming to see her grave. As soon as the Roberts theory became known, Wyoming officials began working toward commemorative markers and dedications. The state of South Dakota, however, argued against this theory. No serious challenges to the Wyoming version developed, however, until well after the middle of the century. For a long time, one historical work dominated scholarship on Sacagawea and perpetuated the myth that she had lived until old age.

The historian Grace Raymond Hebard, who began researching her subject around 1907, finally published in 1933 what would become the definitive work on Sacagawea for decades. *Sacagawea: Guide of the Lewis and Clark Expedition* influenced future historians and novelists alike. Hebard's conclusions were not seriously challenged until the 1960s. Fascinated with the possibility that Sacagawea had living relatives, Hebard interviewed a number of people on the Wind River Reservation and finally concluded that the woman Porivo was indeed Sacagawea.

While it appeared that Hebard had methodically researched and made accurate conclusions, others vehemently argued the opposite. Hebard had obtained a bachelor's degree in engineering and later earned master's and doctoral degrees in political economy. She later served on the board of trustees of the new University of Wyoming when it was first established, and in this way, worked her way into a faculty position there. She ended up in the field of history partly out of political maneuverings in the university and partly because she had a strong interest in the subject. She began publishing works on western history and soon became known as a leading historian of the region.[3]

Like many people before her, Grace Hebard had read a novel by Eva Emery Dye, published in 1902, entitled *The Conquest: The True Story of Lewis and Clark*. Dye was an unusual woman in America at the turn of the twentieth century. She was one of the first generation of American women to graduate from college. She studied literature and poetry and nursed her love of writing for most of her adult life. Although she might have followed a very familiar path of wife and mother in spite of her education, she managed to do more. Her husband was tolerant of a wife who also developed a career, and while raising four children, Dye managed to write many essays and poems, an elementary primer, and four historical novels.

Dye raised her children with her husband in Oregon and became fascinated with the history of the region. She was frustrated that people were ignorant of the history of the north, particularly the Northwest, and she began trying to fill that gap. She was never trained as a historian but conducted exhaustive research about her topics, especially about the Lewis and Clark expedition. She researched document collections, interviewed descendants of Lewis and Clark, and traveled the country in search of the information she needed to make her story both accurate and engaging. She hoped that historical fiction would captivate readers and teach them something about history at the same time.

Like many writers of her generation, Dye was captivated by the Romantics coming out of European centers of literature. American poets, writers, and painters also participated in this movement, characterized by a celebration of emotion, the heroic past, and its larger-than-life characters. When she wrote *The Conquest*, no one had really written anything before about Lewis and Clark outside of academic writing. The book became popular and sparked a strong interest in both the expedition and Sacagawea.[4]

Although historians have criticized Dye's work as biased and a work of American triumphalism, she did conduct research, and her conclusions are not completely inaccurate. However, Dye's work of historical fiction made Sacagawea an almost overnight celebrity after nearly 100 years of obscurity. Suddenly, both historians and amateurs were interested in her story, building statues of her in town squares and trying to lay claim to some part of her past as their own. Dye emphasized Sacagawea's domestic qualities as a wife and mother and her presence on the expedition as a civilizing one. This irony—the native woman civilizing white men—became a rich symbol that Americans loved. Sacagawea was a "savage" who demonstrated the power of the civilizing influence of European culture and its eventual triumph. Like Pocahontas, she also represented a willingness to submit to civilizing influences and turn away from a wilder heritage in the face of obvious progress.

Suddenly, everyone wanted to hear about Sacagawea; the American Indian heroine of the West. She became a guide, not just an interpreter, who helped the United States lay claim to the West. Without her, the story went, Lewis and Clark would have never made it to the Pacific, and American dominion over the West would have been in doubt. Hebard, the engineer/political economist turned historian, read Dye's book and became fascinated by the story of Sacagawea. When in the course of her research she found Reverend Roberts at the Wind River Reservation with his story of Porivo, she was instantly convinced.

A golden rule of historical research is that one should never begin a project with a strong conviction and then search for evidence to support it. While this approach might work with some scientific modes of study, it was entirely detrimental to Hebard's work. Her romantic views of the West, influenced by the works of Dye and others, made her susceptible to the story of Porivo. She wanted Sacagawea to have lived a long life that she could discover and tell. She wanted to talk to and become friends with those who were her descendants and, of course, to honor them in some way. Hebard was not trying to deceive the public with her work. She wanted to believe that what she wrote was accurate and supported by evidence.

Perhaps because she was completely convinced, she was able to convince the reading public, including historians, that Porivo was indeed Sacagawea. At first, other voices did not believe that Porivo was Sacagawea. In 1920, John Luttig's journals were published, and they contained his entry from December 20, 1812, when he recorded the death of "Charbonneau's wife."[5] Hebard read his journal, but because she was already convinced that Sacagawea had lived longer, she decided that this death had been Charbonneau's second wife, whom she called "Otter Woman."[6]

Before Hebard could really participate in the conversation in public, some of the states began vying for the right to claim the suddenly popular Sacagawea as their own. Congressional representatives from both Wyoming and South Dakota argued with each other, one supporting the Luttig journal evidence, and the other Reverend Roberts' claims. To settle the argument, the commissioner of Indian affairs decided to try to solve the controversy. To accomplish this feat, Dr. Charles A. Eastman, a member of the Santee Sioux, was assigned the task of researching Sacagawea's death in 1924. Eastman took his job seriously and began to interview members from the Shoshones, the Gros Ventres, and the Comanches around the region of the Wind River Reservation.

Eastman tried to be thorough, but his two months' worth of interviews produced conflicting stories. In one interview, a Gros Ventre Indian (Mrs. Weidmann) claimed her father had been alive and had met Charbonneau and his two Shoshone wives after the Lewis and Clark expedition. Somehow, Hebard took this as evidence that Charbonneau had taken both of his wives to St. Louis, but left Sacagawea there, and that his other wife died in 1812, not Sacagawea. However, Eastman interviewed another person named Bull Eyes who argued that there was no tradition among his people of Sacagawea. He said he knew of the Lewis and Clark expedition, but if Sacagawea had lived a long life afterward with his people on the Wind River Reservation, her story would be in the oral tradition.

Hebard ignored this interview and only paid attention to the ones she felt supported her theory. She conducted her own interviews and found people who claimed that the woman named Porivo had told them stories of seeing the ocean and a very big fish when she was young. Porivo had a son named Ba'tiz who, in Hebard's view, must have been Jean-Baptiste, or Little Pomp. Hebard wrote her lengthy book claiming Sacagawea had lived as the woman named Porivo until her late eighties. She asserted that Toussaint Charbonneau had been an abusive husband, and that Sacagawea had finally run away from him in the years following the expedition and later went to live on the reservation in Wyoming to be near her people.

There are all kinds of problems with her story, even though books written by historians and novelists alike perpetuated the myth for years afterward. One of the facts that has convinced recent historians to disregard Hebard's conclusions is that Porivo herself never claimed to be Sacagawea and no one had heard that name used during Porivo's life. Another problem is Ba'tiz, who people remember as a very lazy and illiterate man. Jean-Baptiste had received extensive education including five years in Europe. Those who remember him record that he spoke nearly a half-dozen languages fluently. How could this illiterate man named Ba'tiz possibly have been Sacagawea's son?

Hebard explained this problem away by arguing that once Ba'tiz had returned to his people and settled into life on the reservation, he reverted to his old ways, forgetting his education. Unfortunately, Hebard bought into an old stereotype that Native Americans, being naturally "savages," would not retain education once they left a civilized environment. Hebard's argument drew upon many decades of racist assumptions in order to fit her theory.

## A SCHOLARLY BATTLE

Long before mainstream historians began to question Hebard's account of Sacagawea's life, an amateur historian would challenge her in the local newspapers. Blanche Schroer had grown up on the Wind River Reservation. Her father was a physician to the American Indians, and she had always been interested in local history. She was very interested in the Sacagawea/Porivo story and hoped that it was true. However, when she began her own research, she was soon convinced that Hebard had been wrong. She then made it her life commitment to discredit Hebard through documentation. At first, not many people listened. After all, why should an amateur know more than the historian should? Schroer meticulously went through Hebard's research and became more and more convinced that Porivo had not been Sacagawea.

As other scholars would later argue, Schroer found that much of Hebard's oral testimony had been misused. For example, she asserted that Hebard asked people if they had known the woman she was investigating on the Wind River Reservation. They answered yes, and that they knew she had traveled extensively in her long life. However, the testimonials did not mention the name Sacagawea. Schroer claimed that Hebard inserted the name later when she used her testimonials as evidence in her book. The people Hebard interviewed said they knew Porivo, not Sacagawea.[7]

In various articles, newspaper columns, and a book manuscript she never published, Schroer struggled through much of the 1970s to persuade scholars that Hebard had been wrong. She did not blame Porivo, as other had done. Schroer did not believe that Porivo had purposefully claimed to be Sacagawea, but that she had only told stories about her own life.[8] To add proof to her claims, Schroer decided to do more of her own research and found a 92-year-old Shoshone woman from the Wind River Reservation named Jennie Herford Martinez. Herford Martinez said she had known Porivo, who had been her mother's closest friend. They visited almost daily and never once did Herford Martinez remember Porivo talking about traveling with Lewis and Clark, nor did she ever mention the name Sacagawea.[9] Schroer conducted other interviews to further support the argument that Hebard had been wrong. Some of the other people she interviewed told her that they had grown up with Porivo around and that the first anyone had ever heard of Porivo being Sacagawea was after Hebard visited the reservation.

Throughout the rest of her life, Blanche Schroer tried to persuade the state of Wyoming to take down the grave markers erected on the Wind

River Reservation to Sacagawea and Jean-Baptiste. She argued for more than forty years that Porivo had not been Sacagawea. The state of South Dakota liked what Schroer had to say since it supported their assertion that Sacagawea had died there in 1812. Battles over statues and memorials fill Schroer's correspondence, and she worked until she died to challenge Hebard's story. She published a large number of magazine and newspaper articles but never published her manuscript that would tell the true story of Sacagawea.

One of the scholars who regularly corresponded with Schroer and agreed with what she called the "Porivo scam" was historian Irving W. Anderson. A scholar of western history, Anderson never wrote a book about Sacagawea, but he did write many articles and pamphlets about the Lewis and Clark expedition and about Sacagawea and her family. Anderson believed, as did Schroer, that there was no evidence to support the claim that Porivo was Sacagawea. In fact, Anderson very effectively discredited Hebard's research, citing many instances where she read into documents information that simply was not there.[10]

It would appear, then, that Hebard created a fictional Sacagawea just as did novelist Dye. In the face of criticism, Hebard sought documentation to prove her theories for over three decades but never found any. Beyond the statements of two or three people who claimed Porivo had told them she had been with Lewis and Clark, no other evidence ever appeared to support the Hebard theory. On the contrary, evidence that Sacagawea did die at Fort Manuel in 1812 surfaced after Hebard's death in 1836. William Clark made a simple list on the front of his account book for 1825–1828. The list was of all the people who had accompanied him on the expedition to the Pacific, and beside each name, he recorded whether the person was living or dead. Clark wrote: "Se car ja we au Dead."[11] It would have been hard for Hebard to continue arguing her story if there was evidence that Clark believed Sacagawea was dead by 1828.

## LINGERING CONTROVERSY

Not only did Hebard and Eastman popularize the misconception about Sacagawea's death, but they and others also created a virtually mythical character of Sacagawea. Dye's novel really began the process of creating a heroine, an Indian princess, out of the Shoshone interpreter, which is only recently being gently corrected. It is not easy to criticize mythologized people, especially when their stories become major parts of the national dialogue about destiny. From a very early time period in American history, and at least by the middle of the nineteenth century, Americans freely talked about a notion coined Manifest Destiny. This meant that the United States was a unique and important nation, specially blessed by God to grow, become prosperous, and spread across the entire continent.

The phrase *Manifest Destiny* was first coined in 1845 by a popular newspaper columnist named John L. O'Sullivan. A strong proponent of growth and annexation, O'Sullivan argued that God had granted the United States a special role in history—a duty to spread democracy throughout North America. People used this idea to justify the annexation of Texas, and eventually California and the rest of the Southwest. American presidents used the concept to demand control of the Northwest also and would eventually justify expansion beyond the continent in the wake of the Spanish-American War in 1898. By the time Dye wrote her novel about Sacagawea, she and many others viewed Manifest Destiny as the story of America. Sacagawea was a part of that destiny. Without her assistance, the spread of democracy would have been hampered, perhaps even stopped and replaced by British or Russian influences in the Northwest.

Although Sacagawea was an American Indian whose people would be dominated and whose lands would be overrun by the United States, she was "destined" in many ways to assist the process, almost legitimizing it as Pocahontas did for the Jamestown story in 1607. Both American Indian women were elevated to the status of "Indian princess," exceptions to the rule who were more civilized than the rest of their people. These are the notions that came from the concept of Manifest Destiny, especially by the twentieth century. When Hebard wrote her story, she saw Sacagawea as a great heroine of American destiny, almost a tool of divine direction for the United States. Hebard saw her serving in this role with humility and diligence as any good hero or heroine would do.

The only thing wrong with such views of Sacagawea is that scholars came to believe the writings of Hebard as facts, ignoring evidence that Hebard created a character without any documentation. When later historians reexamined this history, they came to realize that there was truly very little known or even knowable about Sacagawea. She lived a short life and played a vital role in the Lewis and Clark expedition, but not as a guide nor as a savior to the men of the corps. Then she died at a young age without any more interesting stories about her life. The only real documents that exist about the life of Sacagawea, the expedition journals, rarely mention her at all. Americans created a Sacagawea who never really existed. The real Sacagawea is much more of a mystery.

Other writers used Sacagawea as a symbol for women, not just of Manifest Destiny. The early twentieth century saw renewed efforts of the women's suffrage movement begun before the Civil War. Women still could not vote in America and had very few legal rights. Protesting this condition, women used Sacagawea as a symbol of strength and of their importance in American history. Even those who published editions of the Lewis and Clark journals in the early twentieth century added commentary about Sacagawea based mostly on works of fiction and upon mythical ideas about Sacagawea. Elliot Coues, one such editor who published the annotated journals in 1893, inserted a lot of commentary about Sacagawea's gentle personality and brave spirit, mostly extrapolated from myth. Dye used this journal edition to write her novel, which later influenced Hebard's work.

For the next several decades after Hebard published her book on Sacagawea, other scholars continued similar arguments about her. While some scholars began to question Hebard's story of Porivo as Sacagawea, most retained the notions that Sacagawea was the most important member of the Lewis and Clark expedition. By the 1940s, however, writers found reasons other than Manifest Destiny for her dedication and self-sacrificing. Many authors began arguing for a romantic relationship between William Clark and Sacagawea. They used some of the commentary Coues made in his edition of the journals about Toussaint Charbonneau. Coues painted him as a cruel and brutal husband, based on the one incident in the original journals when Clark scolded him for hitting his wife. Novelists and others noticed these editorial statements and depicted Sacagawea as a beaten-down woman who naturally fell in love with Clark, a man who was kind to her.[12]

While there is no real evidence of any romantic interest between Sacagawea and any members of the expedition, the supposed romance became part of her legend. One of the popular works of this period about Sacagawea was *Sacajawea of the Shoshones* by Della Gould Emmons, Published in 1943, Emmons accepted Hebard's story of Sacagawea's long life and embellished her work to portray Sacagawea as a heroic American Indian princess who recognized the importance of American civilization and consciously worked to expand its influence. Her love for Clark helped bolster her spirit and resolve. Emmons and others like her argued that Sacagawea was an exceptional person, one of the rare few who could rise above the savagery of her own culture. Naturally, these authors and their readers all assumed that American culture triumphed because it was more advanced, more right, and more blessed.

While much of the myth continued in the same way after the 1960s, views that were more critical appeared in the latter decades of the twentieth century. Both historians and novelists began digging into Sacagawea's story and revising at least parts of the story. Harold P. Howard wrote his work *Sacagawea* in 1971 and sought to be as accurate as possible. He spent considerable space examining the evidence surrounding Sacagawea's death, illustrating how powerful Hebard's claims continued to be. In spite of the power of those claims, however, Howard argued finally that while no definite answers may ever be found, most evidence points to her death in 1812.[13] In spite of Howard's work, Ella E. Clark and Margot Edmonds published *Sacagawea of the Lewis & Clark Expedition* in 1979. In their book, they used the story of Porivo as Sacagawea and seemed to view Hebard's version of her death as fact.[14]

Most works of the 1970s portrayed Sacagawea as a heroine motivated by love. Anna Lee Waldo wrote a wildly popular romance novel entitled *Sacajawea* in 1978, which was reprinted in 1984. Although historians openly criticized the work as terribly inaccurate, the American public kept it on the *New York Times* bestseller list for the better part of a year when it was first published.[15] Waldo used Hebard's story that Sacagawea lived until she was nearly 100 years old. Her portrayal of Sacagawea continued the myth of the American Indian princess who saved the expedition from disaster out of love for William Clark.[16] Very little was written in the 1980s that would reinterpret the traditional myths of Sacagawea.

However, the 1990s would be different. Building upon previous criticisms of the Sacagawea tradition, historians began reexamining both Sacagawea's role on the expedition and how long she may have lived. Some of this work can be explained by the influence of more scholars working in Native American history, including native scholars telling their own stories. Although popular accounts continued portraying Sacagawea as a heroine, others like Donna J. Kessler and Kenneth Thomasma published corrective works in the 1990s. Both argued that the only real evidence of Sacagawea's death is the journal entry of 1812, and that Sacagawea was very helpful to the expedition but had not been its guide.[17]

As recently as 2005, historians continue to counter the effects of Hebard's work. One recent work, Mike Mackey's *Inventing History in the American West*, is exclusively devoted to disproving Hebard's arguments almost point by point. The need to continue arguing against Hebard illustrates the power of her thesis and the strength of the myths about Sacagawea. While many historians no longer discuss Porivo or simply sidestep the issue of when she died, others still argue that she was a guide for the expedition, much more than an interpreter.

As recently as 2008, two other scholars found it important to argue against Hebard's thesis. In their work *Also Called Sacajawea: Chief Woman's Stolen Identity*, Thomas H. Johnson and Helen S. Johnson argue against the theory that Porivo was Sacagawea. In fact, they instead explore

Porivo's true story and conclude that she had been an important American Indian woman in her own right. They assert that Porivo, which meant "Chief Woman" in Comanche, was the wife of Chief Ohamagwaya who signed an important treaty in 1868. In her role as wife of this influential chief, she worked as a diplomat for her people and helped bring the Sun Dance to the Shoshone.[18] The Sun Dance was a collection of ceremonies that were held to connect the people to the Great Spirit. Some of these ceremonies included a dance where young men pierced themselves through the flesh of their chest wall and tied themselves to a pole. As they danced around this pole with the ropes pulling their flesh, they achieved a oneness with the Great Spirit and purification. While many other native peoples practiced this set of ceremonies, the Shoshone had apparently lost this tradition during their years on the reservation. Porivo allegedly brought this ceremony back to the people on the Wind River Reservation. The Shoshones believed that having the Sun Dance traditions brought spiritual rebirth to the Shoshones. Porivo should be remembered for this very important contribution; an accomplishment that was overlooked because Hebard and others mistook her for Sacagawea.

Most other recent works that discuss Sacagawea's story are works that focus primarily on the Lewis and Clark expedition and the lives of members of the expedition after the journey.[19] Other works include a chapter on Sacagawea as an important example of an extraordinary woman in American history, an important person in a larger story, but not eulogized and mythologized as past works have done.[20] In spite of other works written by novelists or other nonscholars who continue to argue in favor of Hebard, most scholars now disregard her arguments.

Although most scholars today do not portray Sacagawea as the American Indian princess guide, the best documents of the journey, the Lewis and Clark journals, do provide a larger picture of Sacagawea than simply an interpreter. However, the mentions of her are scanty and so much has been extrapolated from the few mentions of her in these journals. The American public now thinks that it can own Sacagawea as its national heroine of the West and understand who she really was. There are few people in American history about whom we claim so much with such little evidence. What we know of her life is small, but what we can measure of her myth is very large indeed.

Her real story, as thin as it may be, is still a very interesting one and worthy of remembering. Scholars over the years now seek to uncover the truth about her life, mostly leaving more questions than answers. In many ways, the story of Sacagawea is not just about her life, but also about her myth and what it has meant to Americans over time.

# NOTES

1. Affidavit: "Report on Sacajawea by Reverend John Roberts, Shoshone Mission," January 6, 1936, Blanche Schroer Papers, box 3, folder 8, American Heritage Center, University of Wyoming.

2. Ibid.

3. Mike Mackey, *Inventing History in the American West: The Romance and Myths of Grace Raymond Hebard* (Powell, WY: Western History Publications, 2005), 3–17.

4. Sheri Bartlett Browne, *Eva Emery Dye: Romance with the West* (Corvallis, OR: Oregon State University Press, 2004), 2–6.

5. John C. Luttig, in *Journal of a Fur-Trading Expedition on the Upper Missouri, 1812–1813*, ed. Stella M. Drumm (St. Louis: Missouri Historical Society, 1920).

6. Mike Mackey, *Inventing History in the American West*, 59.

7. Typed Notes, Blanche Schroer Papers, box 3, folder 8, American Heritage Center, University of Wyoming.

8. Notes, Blanche Schroer Papers, box 4, folder 10, American Heritage Center, University of Wyoming.

9. Notes, Blanche Schroer Papers, box 6, folder 5, American Heritage Center, University of Wyoming.

10. Irving W. Anderson, *A Charbonneau Family Portrait: Biographical Sketches of Sacagawea, Jean Baptiste, and Toussaint Charbonneau* (Washington, D.C.: U.S. Department of the Interior, National Park Service, date unknown), 9–11.

11. Anderson, *A Charbonneau Family Portrait*, 10.

12. Donna J. Kessler, *The Making of Sacagawea: A Euro-American Legend* (Tuscaloosa: University of Alabama Press, 1996), 102–103.

13. Harold P. Howard, *Sacagawea* (Norman: University of Oklahoma Press, 1971), 191.

14. Ella A. Clark and Margot Edmonds, *Sacagawea of the Lewis & Clark Expedition* (Berkeley: University of California Press, 1979), 143–44.

15. Kessler, *The Making of Sacagawea*, 149.

16. Anna Lee Waldo, *Sacagawea* (New York: Avon Books, 1979), 562.

17. Kenneth Thomasma, *The Truth about Sacagawea* (Jackson, WY: Grandview Publishing Company, 1997), 91–92.

18. Thomas J. Johnson and Helen S. Johnson, *Also Called Sacajawea: Chief Woman's Stolen Identity* (Long Grove, IL: Waveland Press, 2008), 73.

19. Thomas P. Slaughter, *Exploring Lewis and Clark* (New York: Alfred A. Knopf, 2003); and Larry E. Morris, *The Fate of the Corps: What Became of the Lewis and Clark Explorers after the Expedition* (New Haven: Yale University Press, 2004).

20. Laura McCall, "Sacagawea: A Historical Enigma," in *Ordinary Women, Extraordinary Lives: Women in American History*, ed. Kriste Lindenmeyer (Wilmington, DE: Scholarly Resources, 2000); and Donna Barbie, "Sacagawea: The Making of a Myth," in *Sifters: Native American Women's Lives*, ed. Theda Purdue (New York: Oxford University Press, 2001).

# Chapter 10

# SACAGAWEA'S LEGACY

Whether legend or fact, Sacagawea's story has been told and retold over the last two centuries in American history books and novels, stage productions, and movies. Usually a combination of facts and myths, these stories of Sacagawea have played an important role in the national collective memory. Who she really was is almost not as important as who she became through the commemorations to her over the years.

## STATUES, COINS, AND STAMPS

There are more statues of Sacagawea than any other American woman, past or present. Although it is difficult to know for certain as new statues are erected over time, there are at least 24 statues in different state capitols, parks, and college campuses throughout the country. One of these statues rests in the national capitol, a symbolic recognition of the importance of this native woman to the growth and development of the United States.

Probably the earliest statue of Sacagawea was erected in 1904 in St. Louis, Missouri, for the World's Fair exposition commemorating the Louisiana Purchase. Although it no longer exists, the Bruno Walter Zimm statue became the national visualization of Sacagawea for the future. Photographs of this statue show a beautiful, young American Indian woman, carrying a baby on her back and a walking stick in her hand. She seems stoic and strong, bravely facing whatever might be in front of her. Thus, when Eva Emery Dye wrote her novel *The Conquest*, there was an image people could see in their minds as they read of the American Indian woman who saved the expedition from possible disaster.

In the years following the publication of Dye's novel, many more statues were added. Sculptor Alice Cooper created a bronze statue in 1906, sponsored by the Federated Women's Clubs across the country. It rests in the city park in Portland, Oregon. This statue, apparently influenced by Dye's novel, shows the American Indian woman with a baby on her back, pointing in front of her. This statue clearly reflects the view of Sacagawea as a guide and likely helped to perpetuate this image of her. The most striking part of the statue is her outstretched hand, her face turned forward and upward, seemingly directing the future of America.

Another statue that shows Sacagawea pointing out the way was sculpted by Edwin Cyrus Dallin in 1910. Dallin sculpted many Native American figures, becoming renowned for his work. As a young boy, he grew up in the West and witnessed the Indian Wars and the removal of Plains people to reservations at the end of the nineteenth century. As a young man studying art in Paris, he sketched the American Indians traveling with Buffalo Bill's Wild West Show when it visited France. It is predictable, then, that Dallin's statue of Sacagawea is heroic. In much of Dallin's work, he admittedly sought to portray both realistic figures and idealistic virtues in his subjects. These ideals included patriotism, devotion, dedication, perseverance, and, of course, heroism. Working in the early twentieth century during times of world war and economic depression, it is not surprising that Dallin celebrated these themes in his figures of the American past.

Today, the most famous statue of Sacagawea is a rather old one, sculpted in 1910 by Leonard Crunelle. A French immigrant, Crunelle made the sculpture for the General Federation of Women's Clubs of North Dakota to be placed on the grounds of the state capitol of North Dakota. In this 12-foot-high bronze statue, Sacagawea stands facing westward, baby strapped to her back and face slightly uplifted. Again, one sees a heroic element to the work, and even though she is not pointing, Sacagawea is clearly leading with head up and one foot forward. In 2003, North Dakota funded the making of a replica of Crunelle's statue to be sent to the U.S. Capitol building. It was placed with much ceremony in the National Statuary Hall in October.

Over the years, other statues of Sacagawea have been sculpted and placed around the country. Some of the most interesting ones are group sculptures that feature Lewis, Clark, and Sacagawea. In 1917, Montana artist Charles M. Russell drew a sketch of a proposed sculpture of the three figures for the Society of Pioneers who wanted to commission the sculpture. Although his sketch was never produced exactly, it was used by others to create similar statues patterned after his sketch. In his drawing, Russell depicts two strong pioneers, Lewis and Clark, gazing ahead from a rock. In front of the two men, Sacagawea, with her baby, points the way with an uplifted arm and is stepping forward, but looking back at the two men, beckoning them to follow her. Again, Sacagawea is depicted as a brave American Indian guide.

Finally in the 1950s, artist Henry Lion created a small statue based on Russell's drawing, and another artist, Robert Scriver, created a much larger version in 1976. In Scriver's statue, Sacagawea is seated at the feet of Lewis and Clark, gazing forward as the three figures appear to be studying what is ahead. Although both Russell and Lion depicted Sacagawea pointing, Scriver shows her as just one of three people all perhaps mystified by what they are seeing. This progression of images shows how views of her have changed over time. In recent years, scholars have tried to correct the misconceptions about her, and inevitably, these new views find their way into imagery.

One of the most recent statues of Sacagawea was created by western artist Eugene Daub for Clark's Point overlook of the Missouri River in Kansas City. This statue shows her with Lewis, Clark, York, and the dog Seaman. Daub consulted Shoshone and Hidatsa experts in creating his statue, making sure he captured the look of the clothing and other details as accurately as possible. This statue also shows Sacagawea as an important member of the group but is not the old cliché of her pointing the way for the men. It is a statue that evokes strength and fortitude without glamorizing and romanticizing the American Indian woman. Perhaps this statue is the best depiction of Sacagawea.[1]

In addition to statues, there are many paintings of Sacagawea to add to the imagery. One of the earliest was Charles M. Russell's painting entitled *Lewis and Clark on the Lower Columbia*. This work, painted in 1905, shows Sacagawea with her baby strapped to her back, standing up in a canoe with her outstretched arms supposedly signaling peace to an oncoming canoe of American Indians. This famous work depicted Sacagawea as the peacemaker, an ambassador for the expedition to those they met along the way. Another early depiction was painted by Samuel Paxson in 1906. Again, the centennial of the expedition and the publication of Dye's novel did much to create interest in Sacagawea as a subject of art. In this painting, as in many of the early statues, Sacagawea is with Lewis and Clark, standing slightly in front of them with her hand raised, pointing the way.

In 1993, the U.S. Postal Service issued a postage stamp depicting Sacagawea. This stamp showed a fairly typical-looking American Indian woman with long, black braids, carrying a fairly large cradle board on her back and holding a walking staff in one hand. She is looking off to one side, apparently ready to bravely head forward into the unknown. The image created some controversy over the spelling of her name. Since the government chose to use the traditionally approved spelling of *Sacagawea*, the Shoshone people and others criticized the stamp. They argued that the Shoshone spelling with a *j* would be the correct one, raising once again the issue of ownership of Sacagawea. If spelled with a *j*, then the meaning of her name becomes "boat-pusher" or some equivalent. If spelled with a *g*, then it is something like "bird-woman" and a Hidatsa name. The importance of the name illustrates the significance of her symbolism even today. Both groups wish to claim expertise and special knowledge about Sacagawea, the American Indian woman of the Lewis and Clark expedition.

Another image of Sacagawea has been stamped into gold. In 2000, a special dollar coin was minted with an image of her face and shoulders and the head of Jean-Baptiste on her back. The artist Glenna Goodacre portrayed her as facing away, looking back over her shoulder at the viewer. This direct look is usually not used on coins; most people are shown in silhouette. The coin was issued as another attempt to persuade Americans to adapt to a dollar coin. The first attempt in 1979 was the Susan B. Anthony dollar. It failed, mostly because Americans were slow to give up their paper dollar, and the Anthony coin was easily mistaken for a quarter. The Sacagawea dollar coin was thus stamped with a gold color to help distinguish the coin, but it still remains mostly a collector's item with very limited circulation. Yet it serves as another recent image of Sacagawea, the mother. It is a very personal image and perhaps less romanticized than previous images.

## SACAGAWEA AS ICON AND SYMBOL

What do all these images of Sacagawea really mean? In many ways, Sacagawea as a symbol is just as important as Sacagawea, the real person. Even though we know very little indeed about her actual life, historians, novelists, artists, and so many others have turned her into a national icon representing many things Americans believe about themselves and their past. Sacagawea is an American daughter, adopted from the tribes of "savages" and civilized at least enough to become an important bridge between the colonizers and the native peoples. To many, she became a manifestation of all that is good about American civilization. Its influences could create a heroine out of an untamed people, one who would ensure the success and advancement of that civilization.

There are many kinds of symbols visible in the images of Sacagawea. Not only do the images often portray the incorrect notion that Sacagawea was a guide for the expedition, but they also show other elements. In many of the paintings in which Sacagawea appears, she seems soft, yet brave. She evokes a sense of motherly protection, a tenderness that stands in stark contrast to the rough and tough images of Lewis, Clark, and the other male members of the expedition. Ironically, Sacagawea becomes a civilizing influence on the group. Naturally, she would be a symbol of peace in such a group. In many ways, the documents support the idea that Sacagawea was a symbol of peace. It is very likely that Sacagawea's presence with the corps calmed tensions between the group and the American Indian peoples they met. Portraying this role for her, then, is not at all surprising to see in art and sculpture.

One wonders then, how Sacagawea becomes this important symbol, a heroine for American history, when she was largely absent from history books prior to the late nineteenth century. Since there were very few mentions of her in the journals of Lewis and Clark, almost nothing about her shows up in history texts or novels about the American West until the years approaching the first centennial of the expedition. Years of regional conflict and the Civil War also meant that interpreters of the American past had other heroes to consider. In the years following the war, however, national attention turned to the West as the Plains Indians fought, sometimes won, and ultimately lost their battle to remain free on the open prairie. The end of the Indian Wars with the massacre at Wounded Knee, South Dakota, in 1890 marked a distinct end to an era, one that writers and artists began to commemorate and romanticize as a wild past.

Another important event was the national census in 1890. Once the figures were tallied, it seemed that there was no longer an American frontier, no unsettled wilderness of any great expanse except for Alaska. Historian Frederick Jackson Turner marked the end of the frontier with his "Frontier Thesis" argument, which he presented in 1893. In his paper, he argued that the western frontier had long acted as an important factor in creating a distinct American culture. The encounter with the wilderness, taming it, and carving out a life from it, made Americans uniquely tough, self-reliant, democratic, and superior to the rest of world culture. The West had also served as an important safety valve for the rest of the country, providing space and place for Americans wishing to flee the crowded and immigrant-filled cities of the East. The West provided an abundant supply of natural resources and new markets to spur on the Industrial Revolution in America.

The assumption was that without this endless frontier, American culture might have decayed, with possible consequences to the economy.

Writers and historians naturally looked back into the past for stories about this special interaction with the frontier. No story was as important to this aspect of American history as the Lewis and Clark expedition. In many ways, Sacagawea becomes a symbol justifying Manifest Destiny, the notion popular in the nineteenth century that God had ordained the United States to dominate the continent and spread both Christianity and democracy from sea to shining sea. Sacagawea illustrates the triumph of a superior civilization.

As the centennial approached, writers also looked at the one female member of the expedition with new eyes. Although the Women's Suffrage Movement in the United States had long existed and had not yet gained women the right to vote, it began resurrecting itself in the late nineteenth century. Early twentieth-century women needed a female hero to point to, to illustrate how important women had been to the special American past. Pocahontas and Sacagawea became special heroines in the process. In many ways, this is the beginning of the Sacagawea story in American history. Writers like the novelist Eva Dye and Elliot Coues, editor of an 1893 edition of the Lewis and Clark expedition journals, turned Sacagawea into an Indian princess and heroine.

For Dye, Sacagawea was the perfect historical figure to promote her suffragist views to the American public. An active participant in the suffrage movement, Dye wanted Sacagawea to be seen as the strong and important American woman who saved the expedition from likely destruction. Sacagawea becomes "a model for independent American women" in an age when such models were seemingly few.[2]

Images of American Indians in general were not so favorable in the late 1800s. Throughout American literature up to the early twentieth century, American Indians were portrayed as wild savages in need of taming. In fact, there was no real confidence that "the savage" could actually be tamed. As the reservation system contained more and more of America's native peoples by the end of the nineteenth century, however, more scholars depicted images of the few exceptions to "savagery," and Sacagawea was foremost among them. She could serve, not only as a symbol for women, but as a symbol for the civilizing influence of American culture, an argument that Native Americans could and should be assimilated into the mainstream culture.

In 1887, the General Allotment Act, also known as the Dawes Act, was passed by Congress in an effort to address what was commonly called "the Indian problem." Now that the West was mostly conquered and the American Indians all removed to reservations as eastern tribes had been previously, people began asking questions about what to do next.

American Indians living on the reservations lived desperate lives of poverty, relying on government handouts that often made their way into the hands of corrupt white officials. Would the Indians become permanently dependent upon the government, or could a better way be devised? Some thought that the best answer to the question was to force Indians to become individual property owners.

To solve the problem, the 1887 act broke up the reservations into individual allotments assigned to a single person. In the process, corruption resulted in the theft of much American Indian land, and even those who obtained title lost or sold their land as they failed to make successful farms on it. Reservation land was mostly arid, and inadequate irrigation meant that American Indians who tried to become independent farmers mostly failed at the effort. A new plan to assimilate Indians came from Richard Henry Pratt, a former field officer of the U.S. Army in the West during the Indian Wars of the 1870s and 1880s. Pratt, who also served for a time as jailor of some Indian leaders held in St. Augustine, Florida, came to believe that they could be "civilized" and assimilated through a rigorous education program. He started the Carlisle Indian School in Pennsylvania in 1879 to test his theories.

As years passed, many similar Indian schools were founded across the country, educating young children from the reservations, sometimes taken there by choice, but often by force. The children would be changed into the image of white American culture and taught practical skills to help them integrate into society. Stripped of their culture and language, these children often became lost people, belonging nowhere, never truly accepted by the mainstream culture they were taught to emulate, and abandoned by their native peoples who no longer accepted them. Indian schools, however, continued operating in much the same way well into the twentieth century. Their results for American Indians were mixed at best.

As the Indian schools grew in popularity, images of American Indians in history and literature continued to portray Sacagawea as an exception to the rule, an unusual and heroic character who rose above the backwardness of her people and represented what American Indians could become. In some ways, then, she stood as justification for assimilation programs. With some education, Indians could become as good and beneficial to American society as Sacagawea had been. She was naturally this way without education, representing an innate ability within the Indian to rise above savagery.

These images of Sacagawea persist until midway through the twentieth century. Around the 1940s, writers begin to add to the legend of

Sacagawea and reexamine her story to some extent. Of course, the dominant work of the early twentieth century was historian Grace Raymond Hebard's biography, which claimed that Sacagawea had lived until the late 1800s on the Wind River Reservation in Wyoming. Hebard's work and Dye's novel both perpetuate traditional images of Sacagawea as heroine, guide, and vital member of an expedition out on a divinely sanctioned campaign to conquer the West.

Partly in response to Hebard, historians in the 1940s began looking for evidence to support the story of Sacagawea's long life and many began to see gaping holes. In spite of the criticism, however, Hebard's work continued to sell to libraries and to be held up as the definitive work on Sacagawea through the 1960s. The major difference between modern stories of Sacagawea and nineteenth-century portrayals was the underlying motive. Writers in the 1800s found reasons to argue that Sacagawea believed in the principles of Manifest Destiny and supported the expedition west because she knew it was right. This version helped to justify the conquest of the American West. Mid-twentieth-century writers looked for more human reasons for Sacagawea's heroism. They decided that romance was the answer, and stories of a love relationship between Sacagawea and William Clark proliferated.

Of course, some aspects of the legend did not change. Sacagawea remained an important guide of the expedition, one without whom the journey might have failed. Works written about Sacagawea in the mid-twentieth century thus concentrate more on portions of the story that highlight the personal interaction between Sacagawea and Clark and other members of the corps. These writers wanted to preserve the heroic character without besmirching her reputation, so they emphasized that the love felt between Sacagawea and Clark was never acted on, since she was married. They also portrayed Toussaint Charbonneau as a terrible husband, cruel and unlovable. Sacagawea thus becomes a heroine who perseveres out of love and still remains faithful to an abusive husband.

One of the most powerful genres in which we find Sacagawea as symbol is the motion picture. Beginning with the silent movies of the early twentieth century, American Indians were always portrayed as savages, justifying the conquest of the American West. Well into the 1930s and 40s, such images of Indians persisted in films like *Stagecoach* (1939) and *They Died with Their Boots On* (1941). The popular westerns of the 1950s further spread the image of the wild savage, and the best Indian was a partially civilized sidekick named Tonto who spoke in monosyllables and provided help to those who obviously were his superiors.

*The Far Horizons*, the only Hollywood movie devoted to the Lewis and Clark expedition, was released in 1955, featuring Donna Reed as a white Sacagawea with black braids. Very early in the movie, Charbonneau is depicted as a villain, making it nearly impossible for Sacagawea to resist loving the strong yet tender Clark, portrayed by Charlton Heston. Although panned by critics, the film was fairly popular, and the story of unrequited love irresistible. Sacagawea is a heroine to the expedition out of love and devotion, sacrificing and persevering for the sake of the man she loved. Interestingly, Jean-Baptiste is not featured at all in the movie. His absence made it easier to portray a love affair of the heart while preserving Sacagawea's heroic status.

In the late twentieth century, historians began a period of critical evaluation of all American heroes and symbols. Partly a response to the disillusionment over the Vietnam War and other problems such as the Watergate crisis, historians sought to reinterpret the past by stripping away romanticized images. Works written in the 1970s began to reflect the understanding that not much real evidence existed about Sacagawea at all, and certainly none existed that supported a romance between her and Clark. Others sought to debunk the myth that Sacagawea had actually led the expedition as a guide. They correctly pointed out that the primary task she performed for the expedition was interpreting. They argued she was still an important member of the expedition, but not its savior.

Older images remained, however. As late as 1989, a musical production entitled *Sakakawea* was produced by William Borden and Thomas Peterson. Offered funding by the state of North Dakota for such a production, Borden and Peterson created a modern opera that featured Sacagawea as a brave, heroic woman who saved the corps from inevitable destruction out of love for Clark. The musical also perpetuated the myth that Sacagawea had been Porivo and had lived until old age in Wyoming. Performed as part of North Dakota's centennial celebration of statehood, the musical played before sellout crowds.

Still, the musical did imply that if only Clark had listened to his heart instead of worrying about perceptions of society, maybe he and Sacagawea could have lived a happy life together. This idea carries another message that perhaps if people had acted differently, the story of the West might have been one of joined peoples instead of wars, battles, and reservations. Sacagawea's status as heroine is not simply because she helped the white man's superior culture; she demonstrates her own superiority of emotion, which the playwrights' romanticized as a lost opportunity.

In the late twentieth and early twenty-first centuries, historians and filmmakers like Ken Burns have sought accuracy in their portrayals of

Sacagawea. Since there are few solid details about her life, not many books have been written about her recently claiming to be biographies. Mostly, the story of Sacagawea is the story of the Lewis and Clark expedition with some tantalizing tidbits about this American Indian woman interpreter. Most recent works, then, spend their time discrediting the Porivo story as well as myths about Sacagawea as a guide or as a love interest to Clark. Who she was remains very much a mystery to those who write about her today. The myths, however, are still powerful images that continue to appear in novels, children's literature, and elementary school textbooks.

## SACAGAWEA AND NATIVE AMERICANS TODAY

While it is clear that mainstream Americans have long held Sacagawea as an important heroine, it is less clear how native people view her. This fact is not surprising since Sacagawea aided an expedition of men who claimed ownership of native lands. Is Sacagawea then a villain or simply an unwitting accomplice, forced into her role by circumstances?

Among native people today, there are mixed opinions. Most who have voiced their opinions naturally view the Lewis and Clark expedition as one of conquest and disaster for their people, not something to be celebrated. Fitting Sacagawea into this picture, however, is more complicated. While Sacagawea became an important aid to this expedition of conquest, most native voices heard through oral histories talk about her favorably, and a considerable argument over "ownership" has developed over the past few decades. Instead of addressing whether Sacagawea was culpable or innocent in the conquest of the West, they seek to establish ancestry with her. One Shoshone who did so was Esther Bernett Horne, known to her friends as Essie. In 1989, anthropologist Sally McBeth found Essie and helped coauthor her story. Published in 1998, just a year before her death, the work told a fascinating story of this woman born of a Shoshone mother and white father. As a young woman, she attended Haskell Indian School in Kansas and eventually became a teacher in Oklahoma.[3]

In Essie's case, a Shoshone person not only admired the story of Sacagawea (the Shoshone spell it *Sacajawea*) but even claimed her heritage. Essie's mother grew up on the Wind River Reservation and was told by her mother that she was the great-granddaughter of Sacagawea. Essie grew up with Sacagawea as part of her ancestry. In her discussions with her anthropologist co-author, she examined the argument that Sacagawea died in 1812. To Essie, such an idea was completely false because her Shoshone oral traditions told her otherwise. Sacagawea was a symbol to her also; one of courage, perseverance through difficult times, a heritage to live up to.

Sally McBeth pursued her interest in the Sacagawea story beyond her work with Esther Horne. Interviewing other Shoshone people on the Wind River Reservation, she concluded that most American Indians there accepted the idea that Sacagawea was indeed Porivo who died as an old woman on their reservation. The oral tradition also holds that Sacagawea helped Shoshone Chief Washakie assist her people in adapting to reservation life in the mid-1800s. However, any examination of oral histories recorded prior to Hebard's visit to the region does not include stories of Sacagawea.

On a current Web site for the Eastern Shoshone Tribe on Wind River, there is a story of Sacagawea (Sacajawea) proudly told as part of Shoshone history. It also takes her story beyond the Lewis and Clark expedition to a long life on the Wind River Reservation.[4] Even though the Web site mentions that there is controversy surrounding her later life, her death in 1884 in Wyoming is stated as fact. The Eastern Shoshone of the Wind River Reservation, at least those represented by this Web site, value Sacagawea as part of their history and are proud of her contribution to the Lewis and Clark expedition. The Web site further mentions a statue of Sacagawea erected at the "Sacajawea Cemetery" on the reservation in 2002.

The Lemhi Shoshones of Fort Lemhi Valley Reservation in Idaho feature Sacagawea (Sacajawea) prominently on their Web site.[5] In their description of her life, the Web site reads:

> Without question, Sacajawea (Sacagawea) along with her people and their horses, were the key to the success of the Lewis and Clark Expedition, the greatest exploration of the early American West ever undertaken by a young and struggling country.[6]

The Lemhi Shoshones hold to the generally accepted version of Sacagawea's life, namely, that she died in 1812. They are proud of her heritage and the strength of the American Indian people they believe she represented.

The Comanches also have an oral tradition about Sacagawea. The Wind River story of Porivo held that she had married a Comanche in her later life. This story thus entered Comanche oral history also. Yet, unlike the Wind River Shoshone, the official Web site of the Comanche Nation makes no mention of a connection with Sacagawea.[7] Comanche tribal historian Jimmy Arterberry, however, tells a story his grandmother told him. In this story, Sacagawea traveled south to Comanche land, had a child with a Comanche man, and left the child to be raised with them.[8]

The Hidatsa also have an oral tradition about Sacagawea. In this tradition, found on the Fort Berthold Reservation in North Dakota, Hidatsas argue that Sacagawea (Sakakawea) was actually Hidatsa, not Shoshone. They assert that she and her younger brother Cameahwait were captured by the Shoshone. One day, Sacagawea's adopted Shoshone mother, feeling sorry that she missed her people, helped her escape to return to the Hidatsas. Cameahwait refused to go with her because he had been so young when they were captured and only remembered life with the Shoshones.[9] The official Web site for the Three Affiliated Tribes (Hidatsa, Mandan, and Arikara) at Fort Berthold does have a section they entitle "Sakakawea."

Some Hidatsas reconcile their oral tradition with the Lewis and Clark journals by arguing that translation difficulties were to blame. Lewis and Clark misunderstood what they were told about Sacagawea and did not speak Hidatsa or Shoshone. This explanation seems plausible to most tribal members. In 2001, the Three Affiliated Tribes made an official statement that they believed that Sacagawea (Sakakawea) was indeed of Hidatsa heritage.[10] They claim her as their own.

Not all Shoshone pay much attention to the controversy. Historians Ned Blackhawk and Steven Crum, both western Shoshones, write about the history of their people. Crum does not mention Sacagawea at all in his 1994 work entitled *The Road on Which We Came: A History of the Western Shoshone*.[11] Blackhawk does mention her, but only in passing in his 2006 work entitled *Violence over the Land: Indians and Empires in the Early American West*.[12] Both of these native historians examine more recent histories and concern themselves with life on the reservations and the struggle to retain culture and sovereignty. An argument over ownership of Sacagawea's story is not very important in their research, especially since Sacagawea was eastern, not western, Shoshone.[13]

There are other native writers, however, who have considered the legacy of Sacagawea and written about it in their considerations of the Lewis and Clark expedition. Some of these authors are descendants of native people who met Lewis and Clark and thus grew up hearing about them in their tribal oral histories. Debra Magpie Earling is a member of the Salish and Kootenai Tribes of Montana. Some of her ancestors met Lewis and Clark in 1805 and welcomed them with warm hospitality. She naturally views the expedition as the first stage in a very destructive process of conquest of her people. While she agrees that Lewis and Clark may not have realized the full implications of what their expedition would mean for western American Indians, her view is naturally a very negative one.[14] "In my mind Sacajawea was a traitor," she wrote; "the woman who launched the parade of settlers who would come to claim our land."[15]

Another author, Shoshone-Bannock Mark N. Trahant, finds an inter-esting middle ground between a negative view of the Lewis and Clark ex-pedition and a celebrated ancestral connection. Trahant grew up hearing stories from his grandmother that he was related to William Clark through his great-grandfather, Walter Clark. Trahant did considerable research to see if there was truly a connection, but found no evidence and concluded that there was no way he could have been related to the famous explorer. He does not celebrate this fact, however. Rather, he finds a way to value and preserve his grandmother's story even though it lacks evidence. He, like others, views the expedition as one that would eventually bring many troubles to his people. He also argues that Lewis and Clark had many mis-conceptions about the Shoshones, misunderstanding the measure of wealth among western native tribes and ignoring evidence of a "true" democracy in their political organization.[16] Yet, he still values the place of the expedi-tion in the family stories and considers them an important legacy.

Bill Yellowtail of the Crow nation writes of the Lewis and Clark expe-dition as a significant event that his people need to stop dwelling upon. While it played a major role in the eventual conquest of his people, Yel-lowtail argues that it is time to move on and work on the future.[17] Roberta Conner, of Cayuse, Umatilla, and Nez Perce heritage, also argues that it is time to move on, but she asserts that in order to do so, her people need to remember the legacy of the Lewis and Clark expedition as a lesson in survival. In spite of the catastrophic consequences of the expedition to her people, they still remain and persist in preserving and practicing their cultural values.[18]

In some of these works, Sacagawea is simply not mentioned at all. This might reflect assumptions that she participated in the journey unwillingly or simply unwittingly as an aid to conquest. Keeping their discussions away from her legacy in some ways provides an implicit verdict of in-nocence. Others explicitly discuss her role in the expedition as what an American Indian woman would naturally do for strangers needing help, or as a dutiful wife. Famous Kiowa novelist and poet N. Scott Momaday writes of Sacagawea's courage in the face of danger and her demonstra-tion of courage and fortitude. He envisions Sacagawea as a faithful wife to Toussaint Charbonneau, going on the dangerous journey west because she had been taught to support her husband and to help strangers in need. She can be celebrated as an American Indian woman, in spite of the con-sequences of the expedition she aided. Her story belongs to both main-stream Americans and native peoples.[19]

In the final analysis, Sacagawea's legacy is greater than the sum of its parts. While she did not act as guide to the Lewis and Clark expedition, she provided help and nurture along a difficult trail. The late Vine Deloria, Jr., one of the most respected native historians, wrote that Sacagawea had been the key to the expedition's success. While he mourned its consequences for American Indian people, he celebrated the role Sacagawea played.[20] To Deloria, Sacagawea's story clearly demonstrated that Native Americans were not savages or backward people. They were talented, experienced, courageous, and resilient. In spite of conquest and the loss of their homelands, Native Americans have survived.

Sacagawea, the Shoshone woman of the Northwest, was many things to many people: mother, wife, sister, daughter, gatherer of food, provider of comfort, communicator and ambassador, legend and myth, symbol and legacy. She represents America in ways most people seldom recognize. She belongs to mainstream Americans as an important historical figure and a woman of strength, and she is owned by Native Americans as a symbol of persistence and survival. Few figures of history have made as significant an impact on the collective memory of a people, and with so short a life and so little remaining evidence of how she lived.

# NOTES

1. Albert Furtwangler, *Sacagawea's Son* (Portland: Oregon Historical Society Press, 2004), 10–11.

2. Donna Kessler, *The Making of Sacagawea: A Euro-American Legend* (Tuscaloosa: University of Alabama Press, 1996), 67.

3. Esther Burnett Horne and Sally McBeth, *Essie's Story: The Life and Legacy of a Shoshone Teacher* (Lincoln: University of Nebraska Press, 1998).

4. http://www.easternshoshone.net/EasternShoshoneHistory2.html.

5. http://www.lemhi-shoshone.com/.

6. http://www.lemhi-shoshone.com/.

7. http://www.comanchenation.com/Education/history.html.

8. Sally McBeth, "Memory, History, and Contested Pasts: RE-Imagining Sacagawea/Sacajawea," *American Indian Culture and Research Journal* 27, no. 1 (2003), 16–17.

9. McBeth, "Memory, History, and Contested Pasts: RE-Imagining Sacagawea/Sacajawea," 20; and Gerard A. Baker, "Mandan and Hidatsa of the Upper Missouri," in *Lewis and Clark through Indian Eyes*, ed. Alvin M. Josephy Jr. (New York: Alfred A. Knopf, 2006), 125–36.

10. McBeth, "Memory, History, and Contested Pasts," 21.

11. Steven J. Crum, *The Road on Which We Came: A History of the Western Shoshone* (Salt Lake City: University of Utah Press, 1994).

12. Ned Blackhawk, *Violence over the Land: Indians and Empires in the Early American West* (Cambridge, MA: Harvard University Press, 2006).

13. http://www.temoaktribe.com/history.shtml.

14. Debra Magpie Earling, "What We See," in *Lewis and Clark through Indian Eyes*, ed. Josephy Jr., 47.

15. Josephy Jr., ed., *Lewis and Clark through Indian Eyes*, 45.

16. Mark N. Trahant, "Who's Your Daddy? Lewis and Clark, Told as a Family Story," in *Lewis and Clark through Indian Eyes*, ed. Josephy Jr., 54–56.

17. Bill Yellowbird, "Meriwether and Billy and the Indian Business," in *Lewis and Clark through Indian Eyes*, ed. Josephy Jr., 76–77.

18. Roberta Conner, "Our People Have Always Been Here," in *Lewis and Clark through Indian Eyes*, ed. Josephy Jr., 116–17.

19. N. Scott Momaday, "The Voices of Encounter," in *Lewis and Clark through Indian Eyes*, ed. Josephy Jr., 188–92.

20. Vine Deloria Jr., "Frenchmen, Bears, and Sandbars," in *Lewis and Clark through Indian Eyes*, ed. Josephy Jr., 20–22.

# SELECTED BIBLIOGRAPHY

Adair, James. *History of the American Indians*. 1775. New York: Promontory Press, 1930.

Affidavit: "Report on Sacajawea by Reverend John Roberts, Shoshone Mission," January 6, 1936, Blanche Schroer Papers, box 3, folder 8, American Heritage Center, University of Wyoming.

Ambrose, Stephen E. *Undaunted Courage: Meriwether Lewis, Thomas Jefferson, and the Opening of the American West*. New York: Simon & Schuster, 1996.

Anderson, Irving W. *A Charbonneau Family Portrait: Biographical Sketches of Sacagawea, Jean Baptiste, and Toussaint Charbonneau*. Washington, D.C.: U.S. Department of the Interior, National Park Service, 1988.

Barbie, Donna. "Sacagawea: The Making of a Myth." In *Sifters: Native American Women's Lives*, ed. Theda Purdue. New York: Oxford University Press, 2001.

Bartlett Browne, Sheri. *Eva Emery Dye: Romance with the West*. Corvallis: Oregon State University Press, 2004.

Bergman Peters, Virginia. *Women of the Earth Lodges: Tribal Life on the Plains*. New Haven, CT: Archon Books, 1995.

Blackhawk, Ned. *Violence over the Land: Indians and Empires in the Early American West*. Cambridge, MA: Harvard University Press, 2006.

Blevins, Winfred. *Charbonneau, Man of Two Dreams*. Los Angeles: Nash Publishers, 1975.

Bober, Natalie S. *Thomas Jefferson: Draftsman of a Nation*. Charlottesville: University of Virginia Press, 2007.

Burnett Horne, Esther, and Sally McBeth. *Essie's Story: The Life and Legacy of a Shoshone Teacher*. Lincoln: University of Nebraska Press, 1998.

Carstens, Kenneth C., and Nancy Son Carstens, eds. *The Life of George Rogers Clark, 1752–1818, Triumphs and Tragedies*. Westport, CT: Praeger, 2004.

Clark, Ella A., and Margot Edmonds. *Sacagawea of the Lewis & Clark Expedition*. Berkeley: University of California Press, 1979.

Colby, Susan M. *Sacagawea's Child: The Life and Times of Jean-Baptiste (Pomp) Charbonneau*. Spokane, WA: Arthur H. Clark Company, 2006.

Cole Trenholm, Virginia, and Maurine Carley. *The Shoshonis: Sentinels of the Rockies*. Norman: University of Oklahoma Press, 1964.

Coues, Elliott, ed. *History of the Expedition under the Command of Lewis and Clark*. 1893. 3 vols. New York: Dover Publications, 1965.

Crum, Steven J. *The Road on Which We Came: A History of the Western Shoshone*. Salt Lake City: University of Utah Press, 1994.

Defenbach, Byron. *Red Heroines of the Northwest*. Caldwell, ID: The Caxton Printers, 1929.

Emery Dye, Eva. *The Conquest: The True Story of Lewis and Clark*. 1902. New York: Binfords & Mort Publishers, 1936.

Farnsworth, Frances J. *Winged Moccasins: The Story of Sacagawea*. New York: J. Messner, 1954.

Fenaison, Edward, and Mel Gemmill. *Sacagawea: A Life beyond Expectation*. East Helena, MT: E & M Books, 2004.

Furtwangler, Albert. *Sacagawea's Son*. Portland: Oregon Historical Society Press, 2004.

Glancy, Diane. *Stone Heart: A Novel of Sacajawea*. New York: Overlook Press, 2003.

Gould Emmons, Della. *Sacajawea of the Shoshones*. Portland, OR: Binfords & Mort, 1943.

Hall, Brian. *I Should Be Extremely Happy in Your Company: A Novel of Lewis and Clark*. New York: Viking Press, 2003.

Hebard, Grace R. Grace Raymond Hebard Papers. American Heritage Center, University of Wyoming, Laramie, Wyoming, n.d.

———. *Sacajawea: A Guide and Interpreter of the Lewis and Clark Expedition, with an Account of the Travels of Toussaint Charbonneau, and of Jean Baptiste, the Expedition Papoose*. 1932. Glendale, CA: Arthur H. Clark Company, 1967.

Howard, Harold P. *Sacagawea*. Norman: University of Oklahoma Press, 1971.

Jackson, Donald, ed. *Letters of the Lewis and Clark Expedition with Related Documents, 1783–1854*. Urbana: University of Illinois Press, 1978.

Johnson, Thomas J., and Helen S. Johnson. *Also Called Sacajawea: Chief Woman's Stolen Identity*. Long Grove, IL: Waveland Press, 2008.

Josephy, Alvin M., Jr., ed. *Lewis and Clark through Indian Eyes*. New York: Alfred A. Knopf, 2006.

Jung, Patrick. "The Creation of Métis Society: French-Indian Intermarriage in the Upper Great Lakes." *Voyageur* (Winter/Spring 2003), 43.

Kessler, Donna J. *The Making of Sacagawea: A Euro-American Legend.* Tuscaloosa: University of Alabama Press, 1996.

Lamb, Sydney. "Linguistic Prehistory of the Great Basin." *International Journal of American Linguistics* 24 (1956): 95–100.

Lowie, Robert H. "The Northern Shoshone." In *Anthropological Papers of the American Museum of Natural History.* New York: Trustees of the American Museum of Natural History, 1909.

———. "Notes on the Social Organization and Customs of the Mandan, Hidatsa, and Crow Indians." In *Anthropological Papers of the American Museum of Natural History.* New York: Trustees of the American Museum of Natural History, 1917.

Luttig, John C. In *Journal of a Fur-Trading Expedition on the Upper Missouri, 1812–1813*, ed. Stella M. Drumm. St. Louis: Missouri Historical Society, 1920.

Mackenzie, Alexander. *Voyages from Montreal on the River St. Laurence throughout the Continent of North America, to the Frozen and Pacific Oceans in the Years 1789 and 1793.* Ann Arbor, MI: University Microfilms, 1966.

Mackey, Mike. *Inventing History in the American West: The Romance and Myths of Grace Raymond Hebard.* Powell, WY: Western History Publications, 2005.

Mann, John W. W. *Sacajawea's People: The Lemhi Shoshones and the Salmon River Country.* Lincoln: University of Nebraska Press, 2004.

McBeth, Sally. "Memory, History, and Contested Pasts: RE-Imagining Sacagawea/Sacajawea." *American Indian Culture and Research Journal* 27, no. 1 (2003): 1–32.

McCall, Laura. "Sacagawea: A Historical Enigma." In *Ordinary Women, Extraordinary Lives: Women in American History*, ed. Kriste Lindenmeyer. Wilmington, DE: Scholarly Resources, 2000.

McMurtry, Larry. *Sacagawea's Nickname: Essays on the American West.* New York: New York Review Books, 2001.

Milligan, Stephanie, Grace Steele Woodward, Harold P. Howard, and Gae Whitney Canfield. *Three American Indian Women: Pocahontas, Sacajawea, and Sarah Winnemucca of the Northern Paiutes.* New York: MJF Books, 1995.

Morris, Larry E. *The Fate of the Corps: What Became of the Lewis and Clark Explorers after the Expedition.* New Haven, CT: Yale University Press, 2004.

Moulton, Gary E., ed. *The Journals of the Lewis and Clark Expedition.* Lincoln: University of Nebraska Press, 1983–2001. Also available at http://lewisandclarkjournals.uw.edu/index.html.

Nelson, W. Dale. *Interpreters with Lewis and Clark: The Story of Sacagawea and Toussaint Charbonneau.* Denton: University of North Texas Press, 2003.

*Placer Herald*, Auburn, California, Placer County Auburn Public Library, July 7, 1866.

Porter, Roy. *The Greatest Benefit to Mankind: A Medical History of Humanity from Antiquity to the Present*. New York: Harper Collins, 1997.

Purdue, Theda, ed. *Sifters: Native American Women's Lives*, 13 vols. Chapel Hill: University of North Carolina Press, 2000.

Rees, John E. *Madame Charbonneau: The Indian Woman Who Accompanied the Lewis and Clark Expedition, 1804–6. How She Received Her Indian Name and What Became of Her*. Salmon, ID: Lemhi Country Historical Society, 1970.

Reid, Russell, and Larry Remele. *Sakakawea: The Bird Woman*. Bismarck: State Historical Society of North Dakota, 1986.

Ronda, James P. *Lewis & Clark among the Indians*. Lincoln: University of Nebraska Press, 1984.

———. *Thomas Jefferson and the Changing West*. St. Louis: Missouri Historical Society Press, 1997.

Schoer, Blanche. Blanche Schoer Papers. American Heritage Center, University of Wyoming, Laramie, Wyoming, n.d.

Schultz, James W. *Bird Woman*. New York: Houghton Mifflin, 1918.

Slaughter, Thomas P. *Exploring Lewis and Clark*. New York: Alfred A. Knopf, 2003.

Stewart, Frank H. "Hidatsa." In *Handbook of North American Indians*. Washington, D.C.: Smithsonian Institution, 2001, 13:1, 334–35.

Sundquist, Asebrit. *Sacajawea & Co. The Twentieth-Century Fictional American Indian Woman and Fellow Characters: A Study of Gender and Race*. Oslo: Solum Forlag, 1991.

Taylor, Frederick. *Pomp: The Long, Adventurous Life of Sacagawea's Son*. Bloomington, IN: AuthorHouse, 2004.

Thomasma, Kenneth. *The Truth about Sacagawea*. Jackson, WY: Grandview Publishing Company, 1997.

Wade, Ira O. *The Intellectual Origins of the French Enlightenment*. Princeton, NJ: Princeton University Press, 1971.

Waldo, Anna L. *Sacagawea*. New York: Avon Books, 1979.

Walker, Deward E., Jr. "A Revisionist View of Julian Steward and the Great Basin Paradigm from the North." In *Julian Steward and the Great Basin: The Making of an Anthropologist*, ed. Richard O. Clemmer, Daniel Myers, and Mary Elizabeth. Salt Lake City: University of Utah Press, 1999.

Wilson, Gilbert L. *Buffalo Bird Woman's Garden: Agriculture of the Hidatsa Indians*. 1917. St. Paul: Minnesota Historical Society, 1987.

Wood, Raymond W., and Thomas D. Thiessen. *Early Fur Trade on the Northern Plains: Canadian Traders Among the Mandan and Hidatsa Indians, 1738–1818*. Norman: University of Oklahoma Press, 1985.

Woodward, Tim. "Sacajawea: Her Story by Her People." *Idaho Statesman*, January 3, 2003.

Worley, Ramona C. *Sacajawea, 1788–1884: Refuting Evidence to the Contrary.* Fort Collins, CO: Business Express, 2006.

## WEB SITES

Barbara Goodin, "Comanche Nation History": http://www.comanchenation.com/Education/history.html

The Eastern Shoshone Tribe, Fort Washakie, Wyoming: http://www.easternshoshone.net/EasternShoshoneHistory2.html

The Lewis and Clark Trail: http://www.lweisandclarktrail.com/newfoundland.htm

Lewis and Clark, Public Broadcasting Corporation: http://www.pbs.org/lewisandclark/inside/wclar.html

The Official Site of the Fort Lemhi Indian Community: http://www.lemhi-shoshone.com

Te-Moak Tribe of the Western Shoshone Indians of Nevada: http://www.temoaktribe.com/history.shtml

# INDEX

## About the Author

APRIL R. SUMMITT is Assistant Professor of History at Arizona State University's Polytechnic Campus. She has published and presented several articles, book entries, reviews, and papers in the areas of Native American history, western American history, the ethnohistory of Appalachia and the American South, and the cultural history of river environments. Her current research focuses on a comparative analysis of Cherokee and Anglo-American mappings of space and place.

www.ingramcontent.com/pod-product-compliance
Lightning Source LLC
Chambersburg PA
CBHW070442100426
42812CB00004B/1184